RIGHT FROM THE START!

CALLING EVANGELICAL LEADERSHIP TO FAITH IN GENESIS 1–2

David M. Fouts, B.A., Th.M., Th.D.

ISBN-13: 978-0692588208 (Courthouse Printers)

ISBN-10: 0692588205

Table of Contents

Forward

Every generation of the Church and of biblical scholarship with it seems to face new issues of such importance that if left unanswered threaten to bring shipwreck to the historic Christian faith. This day and age is no different. This time, an old conflict generated by the Darwinian evolutionary world view has come back with a zeal but the situation now is quite different. Then virtually the whole world of conservative scholarship was arrayed against the notion of a mechanistic and mindless progression of natural processes resulting at last in *homo sapiens* in all its mysterious wonder. Now it is not the secular mindset alone that sets itself against the biblical witness concerning origins, but an entire guild of evangelicals that have joined forces with the skeptics and are raising serious doubts about the historicity and scientific validity of the very texts that set the stage for the historic Christian understanding of creation, sin, and redemption as historical facts.

David Fouts has sounded the alarm of warning and offered a counter and persuasive response in this well researched and well thought-out treatise. He shows the hollowness of parroting long discredited proposals offered by previous generations of secularists and wonders how it is that the same old paradigms that could not undermine the biblical tradition then are being raised from the death of irrelevance by moderns within Evangelicalism who are trying to breathe into it the breath of life. Surely the sage was correct in observing that "There is nothing new under the sun."

Fouts is an important read for anyone interested in noting trends in contemporary evangelical scholarship.

Eugene H. Merrill
Distinguished Professor of Old Testament Interpretation
The Southern Baptist Theological Seminary
Louisville, KY

Abbreviations

ANE Ancient Near Eastern
BDB Brown, Driver, and Briggs
BHS *Biblia Hebraica Stuttgartensia*
CTA *Corpus des tablettes en cunéiformes alphabétiques*
ICC International Critical Commentary
KJV King James Version
LXX Septuagint
MT Masoretic Text of the Hebrew Bible
NASV New American Standard Version
NIV New International Version
NT New Testament
OT Old Testament

Acknowledgements

The printed form of this book has been a long time coming. I am very pleased that it is drawing to an end. Any published author will admit that a lot of life occurs during the research and writing of a book, and that there are always things that make one say, "I wish had written this," or "I should have omitted that." In that sense, writing a book is done much in the same way that we play life. We do/say/write what we think we must, and leave the outcome to a providential God, perhaps to be undone/redone/edited in the future. Or not.

That being said, I need to be grateful to King Jesus for certain people He has brought alongside me for the journey. Earliest perhaps is that thanks should be offered to Dr. Kurt Wise, former colleague at Bryan College, who first brainstormed with me about the direction the book should take. Lt. Colonel David Johnston, also a former colleague at Bryan, has been cheering from the sidelines for many years, offering manifold suggestions on earlier drafts, and the first to order hard copies. John May, former pastor in McMinnville, Tennessee, whom God brought alongside to encourage me to continue the task at about the 80 percent mark, needs to recognize what a God-send he really was. Michael Heiser, my former student in beginning Hebrew many years ago at Dallas Seminary, has always remained one of the most caring and understanding brothers in Christ, and published the earliest edition of *Right from the Start* as an e–Book at Logos.com two years ago. My son-in-law, Todd Havener, has been very valuable in support and in helping to orchestrate the process of the first printed edition. My first cousin, Cindy Strong Hart, saved me time, money, and honor in her service to me as a professional proofreader. To paraphrase the apostle Paul, "I give thanks to my God for my every remembrance of all of you!"

Right from the Start!

It is my highest privilege to give thanks to God for my family as well. My dear wife, Esther, helps to keep me both sane and focused, and does so with mercy, grace, and laughter. Leanne Havener, our daughter, is the most ardent supporter of me as her stepdad and as Papa Dave to her two sons Cameron and Rylan. My own children Jason and Heidi are great blessings to me, and I love them dearly. My grandson Jackson will be happy with me no matter what, and for that I am most humbly grateful.

Introduction

Nothing could be more exciting for a twelve-year-old boy than to spend a week or so at Worth Ranch, the Boy Scout camp on the banks of the Brazos River just north of Palo Pinto, Texas. The combination of water, trees, cactus, caves, cliffs, and other neat stuff, combined with being away from home — especially away from my three sisters (all of whom I love very dearly today!) — well, at that time I was beside myself with excitement!

After jumping out of the vehicles that were barely stopped, we stowed the gear in our assigned tents, and began bounding about like wild men, waiting for some direction to the fun. Our excitement, which was no doubt partially due both to adrenalin and to the onset of puberty for many of us, was channeled by our scoutmaster leading us on a pre-dinner hike up Split Rock Mountain. Rising up probably 200 or 300 feet above the Brazos below, it was for most of us (from the mostly flat Ft. Worth area) an amazing facet of creation. It appeared to my young and inexperienced eyes to be made of … rock (it was limestone, I think), covered over with various kinds of vegetation. On one end, and easily visible from our campsite, a pillar of rock had sometime in the distant past separated from the main cliff by a distance of four or five feet, hence the name Split–Rock. The gap between was quite deep, but talented young athletes would dare the challenge, leaping from one side to the separated ledge and back again.

Crossing a small waterless creek, and surrounded everywhere by prickly pear cactus and junipers, we began our trek upward, startled occasionally by the sound of some critter either bouncing off or slithering through the vegetation. The trail appeared to be mostly loose gravel of some type, and as I walked I found some interesting items in the pathway. These discoveries seemed to be very plant-like in shape, sort of like a straw, but sectioned off in pieces less than two inches in length. They had an interesting design at each end and were made out of the ubiquitous rock (limestone). My scoutmaster answered my youthful query by responding that I had found fossils from millions of years ago, fossils of an ancient marine animal known to paleontologists as a *crinoid*.

Two amazing things had just been presented to me. First, I had found on the side of a mountain, with my very own twelve-year-old eyes, the remains of an animal that looked like the stem of a plant, which at one time lived in the ocean. I could handle that. I knew of the story of Noah's flood. We had been taught at church that the flood had covered the entire planet, so a mountain in north central Texas would have been certainly submerged, I had thought at the time. The second thing was that my trusted scoutmaster had told me was that it was millions of years old. This new knowledge troubled me, since I had also been taught by my church that the earth was not millions of years old but rather only several thousand. Given the severity of the shock that this new information gave me, and the gravity of the issues involved, I did what any reasonably intelligent twelve-year-old boy enjoying his first trip to scout camp would do: I simply ignored the conflict in my mind, suppressing it for another day.

Fast-forward seven years. Though I had been in church most of my life, I actually did not trust Jesus as God's provision for forgiving my sin until I was nineteen and away at college. Immediately following my conversion to Christ, a hunger for God's Word began in me in earnest. Besides reading the Bible completely during the first two months after salvation, I also began reading books about the Bible.

A friend, though I cannot remember whom, introduced me to *The Genesis Flood,* published in 1961 and written by Old Testament scholar John Whitcomb and highly degreed civil engineer Henry M. Morris. In a nutshell, this book argued that the fossil record observable in the geologic column was, in effect, the results of the global flood recorded in Genesis 6–9, and therefore the earth probably was not millions of years of age, as my scoutmaster had assured me years before. Wow! The internal struggle I had felt, and then suppressed, at Scout Camp came back strongly. So I did what any self–respecting college student with all the extracurricular activities, with Navigators, Campus Crusade, Baptist Student Union would do: I suppressed it again.

Fast-forward seven years. The Lord, after saving me and filling me with a passion to know Him through prayer and through His Word, called me to seminary in order to serve Him full time in what I thought was to be a pastoral ministry. I actually sat under the teaching of the esteemed scholar Dr. Bruce Waltke for a course entitled Biblical Introduction during what was to be his final year at Dallas Seminary. Dr. Fred Howe was also then at Dallas, a delightful professor of theology, so much so that we called him "Frederick the Gracious." He had chosen the text *Man's Origin, Man's Destiny* by A. E. Wilder–Smith for our class on anthropology. As I recall, this book was young–age creationist in perspective, appropriate for the Dallas faculty at that time, all of whom as I understood it then held to that perspective. So instead of suppressing the tension between the Scripture and the findings of science, I embraced the young earth position and lived with the new tension that that decision produced.

Fast-forward seven more years after graduating with my Th.M. in Old Testament Literature and Exegesis. I journeyed to Montana and Idaho, where I served two pastorates, started a professional courier business, and taught at Yellowstone Baptist College. God called me back for further education, and try as I might to go elsewhere for my doctorate (per the conventional wisdom that promoted a divergent education), I was constrained by the providence of God to return to Dallas. Much had changed at Dallas in the interval, and though most there were still young earthers, I had too much to do in the doctoral program to really engage in potential debates over the age of the earth. Yet, God was preparing me in the field of Old Testament studies to do just that.

Fast-forward yet another seven years. Kurt Wise and I met my first year at Bryan College. Kurt is an amazing individual whom I am proud to name as a choice friend, and a committed young earth proponent. Highly credentialed, he has degrees from the University of Chicago and Harvard University, at the latter of which he earned his Ph.D. in Invertebrate Paleontology under famed evolutionist, the late Stephen J. Gould. To say that Kurt is intelligent and well educated would be an understatement, and God is using him mightily for the cause of young earth creationism around the world.

Fast-forward fourteen years. I am proud to say that I was also Kurt Wise's professor of Hebrew at Bryan College, and that he was an excellent student for one semester. Unlike most college students, Kurt learned enough in one semester to continue viable study on his own. Early on in our friendship, I sensed that God was leading us into a very close working relationship, which continues today, though he is now at another college and I am no longer at Bryan. Though I had been ruminating on this current project for many years, it was a 2007 encounter with Kurt at the annual meeting of the Evangelical Theological Society that convinced me to write this book.

Right from the Start!

Evangelical leadership is at a critical crossroads in the United States. A recent Zoomerang Poll (2009), conducted by Dr. Bruce Waltke of Regents College of Vancouver, BC, and also Reformed Seminary in Orlando, Florida, at that time, demonstrates this crisis among evangelical academia.[1] In an attempt to ascertain what the typical evangelical academic believes about the young earth versus old earth debate, Waltke made his twelve question ballot available to evangelical seminary professors.[2] The ballot was simple, as one needed only to press the radio button for an affirmative answer, with no button push indicating a negative answer. Of 659 who visited the restricted site, only 264 completed the survey. It would be difficult to ascertain at this point why those who did not complete the survey chose not to do so.

The twelve questions were offered to explore the barriers evangelicals find to harmonizing the Scriptural account with Darwinian evolution. These questions are listed below:

1. The creation accounts of Genesis 1 and 2, when interpreted by the grammatico–historical method, cannot be harmonized with creation by the process of evolution.

2. The creation accounts of Genesis 1 and 2 and the genealogies of Genesis 5 and 11 cannot be reconciled with the extended period of time demanded by creation by means of an evolutionary process.

3. God's sentence of death and decay on the creation in connection with Adam's fall cannot be harmonized with the theory of creation by the process of evolution.

4. The theory of creation by the process of evolution does not harmonize with the doctrine of Adam's headship over the whole human race.

5. The Institute of creation Research, founded by Henry Morris, has presented sufficient scientific evidence to reject the theory of creation by the process of evolution.

---

[1] Bruce Waltke, "Barriers to Accepting the Possibility of Creation by Means of an Evolutionary Process," *Biologos*, Dec. 2011 (biologos.org/uploads/projects/Waltke_scholarly_essay.pdf), 1–10.

[2] The schools chosen were all led by members of the Fellowship of Evangelical Seminary Presidents. These include up to some eighty school presidents fellowshipping together for the past thirty years or so. This fellowship has no website of which I am aware.

6. The Reasons to Believe Ministry, represented by Hugh Ross, has presented sufficient scientific evidence to reject the theory of creation by the process of evolution.

7. Apologists such as those of the Intelligent Design Movement, fathered by Phillip E. Johnson, have made a sufficient case to reject the theory of evolution and to replace it with a theory of intelligent design.

8. Ken Ham rightly argues "Scientists only have the present—they do not have the past," ruling out the possibility of science to theorize the history of origins.

9. The apparent age of the universe can be explained by reckoning that God created the universe with apparent age.

10. The Gap Theory (i.e., the destruction of an original creation explains the geological/fossil record) hinders me from accepting the theory of creation by evolution.

11. The Framework hypothesis (i.e., the days of Genesis are artistically arranged and not literal) hinders me from accepting the theory of creation by evolution.

12. None of the above. I can accept the theory of theistic evolution.

That this survey could be improved is admitted by Waltke.[3] Nevertheless, it is extremely revealing first of all in that the issue is not a dead issue at all but very alive and persevering, even in evangelical academia. Too, the great number of non-respondents may or may not be disturbing, depending on those who did not wish to take sides on the issue for whatever reasons. More disturbing to the present author, however, is the result of the survey that shows so few evangelical academics (44 percent) chose the simple accounts of Genesis 1 and 2 as authoritative over evolution on the issue of the origins of the heavens and the earth. In contrast, 46 percent chose the radio button affirming that they can accept the theory of theistic evolution![4]

---

[3] Waltke, 3, 10.

[4] Waltke, 7.

Never in my wildest dreams could I have imagined that the recent creation of the heavens and the earth as described in Genesis 1–2 would have been challenged, not just by the claims of Darwinian evolution, which I expected, but by the unanticipated equivocations by contemporary brothers and sisters in the faith. And these are the professors in our evangelical seminaries to whom the modern church entrusts our most promising young leaders!

This is particularly, and dishearteningly, seemingly true of the majority of evangelical leadership in the United States. One may excuse, to a certain extent, evangelical scientists, mathematicians, and other untrained or minimally trained in biblical studies to succumb to the avalanche of public and scientific opinion favoring an old earth. But, the heartbreaking evidence seems to show that well-trained evangelical leadership involved in biblical studies, Christian college administrations, pastorates, and para-church organizations have also succumbed.

Many recent scholarly works by well–educated Hebraists and popular theologians nearly all seem to waffle when it comes to the age of the earth. College and seminary administrations, in an effort to get the "best" employee for a given position, hire presidents and vice–presidents who either are openly old earth, or don't consider the issue of great importance in their curricula.[5] Many pastors, in an effort to be "seeker friendly," simply ignore teaching concerning the origins of the universe by overlooking Genesis 1–2 in their homilies, sermons, and expositions. Numerous leaders of para–church organizations, many of whom formerly stood fast on young earth positions, have found that "broadening their base" is easier when they take no official position. This disturbing shift is not because the text is

[5] One doubts that there are more than ten accredited Christian colleges, graduate schools, or seminaries in the Western Hemisphere that would openly claim that they have a young earth perspective. The number ten is probably too high, as the great majority either do not take a position or are clearly old earthers.

not clear but rather that it is very clear. Yet the traditional understanding that the earth was created in six literal days does not square well with the empirical data as interpreted by numerous scientists.[6] In fact, due the dearth of strong, scholarly voices of those well trained in biblical Hebrew to develop a biblical model of a recent creation, many evangelical scientists have attempted to develop their own models of an old earth, with varied results.[7] Very few take a strong public stand in favor of the young earth position.

On the other hand, many (I think most) evangelicals in the pew and in the classroom, certainly many in Christian homes, continue to believe the simple truth that our God, the God of the Bible, did indeed create the heavens and the earth and all that they contain in their entirety in six days. After all, Exodus 20:11 states: "For in six days the Lord made the heavens and the earth and the sea and all that are in them." In light of "modern empirical observations of the universe," why would anyone continue to believe such a thing? Perhaps it is because we value the Scriptures as God's authoritative Word, and we recognize that the clear teaching of Genesis 1–2 reflects this belief as truth.

God's Word alone should trump the interpretation of modern empirical data from the so-called "Book of creation,"[8] but doesn't always do so in the understanding of many in today's world. In fact, so many of our evangelical leaders have simply abandoned the discussion that few, if any, Christian colleges, universities, or seminaries today take an

---

[6] One evangelical professor from a well–known seminary recently emailed me that: "I have to admit, however, that with all the apparent discontinuities between modern empirical observation of the cosmos (general revelation, if you will) and Genesis 1, I am surprised that you want to view the latter as scientific."

[7] It is the nature of the case that for one such as I to comment with any authority on any field of science, say biology or astronomy, would be to commit the logical fallacy of appeal to misplaced authority. On the other hand, the church seems to allow many evangelicals formally trained in scientific fields to comment freely in public forums, from the pulpit, and in print, on the Hebrew text of Genesis. Often, these go uncensored by church leadership, even when their statements actually contradict the clear statements of the Bible. This perhaps is evidence of the inordinately high regard we place on science and on the scientific community.

[8] The so called "Book of Creation" is a non-biblical term meant by many to simplify the theological concept of general revelation.

official stand on the issue of young earth versus old earth.[9] Therefore, this is my challenge to the evangelical leadership of the universal church of Jesus Christ that they come to faith in Genesis 1–2 as an integral and essential part of the authoritative Word of God. I call upon you as individuals to believe the clearly stated words, to be consistent in hermeneutics, to understand the full ramifications that disbelief would have for the Christian faith, for *our* faith in our Redeemer, the King of Kings, Jesus the Messiah.

As I write these words, the 200th anniversary of the birth of two individuals very significant in the development of Western Civilization has recently been celebrated in 2009. These are, of course, Abraham Lincoln and Charles Darwin. Too, 2009 was the 150th anniversary of the publication of Darwin's *Origin of Species*. Therefore, there seems to be no better time than now to write this book as an *apologia* (defense) for the young earth perspective, a perspective that I and numerous others believe is the result of an inductive exegesis of the words of the authoritative Scriptures.

I write these words as well for the church universal of Jesus Christ, the body of called-out believers who depend on His Spirit and His Word to guide them now and for eternity. I write for those in the classroom and in the pew who are looking to evangelical leadership to be consistent with their hermeneutics (method of interpretation). I write this book because there have been so many who have not wished to take a stand for the authority of the Word of God against the widely held doctrines of Darwinism and its aftermath. Many have fled the battlefield of biblical and theological debate. I prefer to take my stand on the frontlines.

---

[9] As an example, the college at which I most recently served, though known for years as a strong young earth institution, had recently hired a vice president of academics who did not consider the issue academically important. More recently, the results of this thinking have ushered in devastating consequences of disharmony and turmoil.

To take the position I understand the Scriptures to be taking, the position I take to be factual, is very much like a modern age David facing an ideological Goliath. Instead of taking up the ill–fitting armor of Saul, which may be represented today by scientific acumen, I take instead that which fits well, that with which God has provided me: the Word of God. My five smooth stones are to be found in the broad education offered by numerous years of study for both the Th.M. and Th.D. degrees in biblical Hebrew and Old Testament studies at a fully accredited and well-respected seminary, numerous publications and national presentations centered in Genesis 1–2, as well as my nearly twenty years of teaching the same on both the undergraduate and graduate levels.

My method will not be exhaustive, in the sense that not every scholar who has commented on the text will be analyzed. Rather, it will focus on the words, constructions, structures, and issues that feed the debate between those who hold to a young earth (or, recent creation) and those who hold to an old earth. My prayer is that this work will be both scholarly and understandable not only to evangelical leadership who have already capitulated to the so–called "irrefutable conclusions of modern empirical observations" but also to the interested layperson. For the modern day church of Jesus the Messiah, this is my report from the frontlines of the battle, based in the front pages of the authoritative Word of God, and from the front of time. It is my hope as well that God will use this work to restore evangelical Christians back to a faith position that affirms Genesis 1–2 as an integral and foundational part of the authoritative Word of God, and in so doing, recognize that the traditional understanding has been right from the start. May God bless His Church and you personally through my *apologia*.

One: The Authority of the Bible

Bill O'Reilly is the host of the *O'Reilly Factor*, ostensibly the highest-ranked cable news program in America. On one of his weeknight broadcasts (late February or early March of 2013), Mr. O'Reilly eschewed the literal interpretation of Genesis 1, understanding that key passage as "allegorical." When asked by one of his listeners to explain why he held that position, he responded "SCIENCE" with emphasis that I perceived indicated his viewpoint that science was the final word on the subject. In a similar discussion earlier during 2012 with Bernie Goldberg, Mr. O'Reilly agreed with Mr. Goldberg that those who believe in a literal account in Genesis 1 were, as I remember the term, "ignorant." Though I have sent numerous emails politely objecting to both his hermeneutics and to his ad hominem attacks on those who consider the authority of Scripture weightier than the authority of science, Mr. O'Reilly has not yet responded to me. That is okay. I don't need his approbation. How's that for the word of the day, Bill?

One doesn't hear from pulpits much anymore about the Bible as the Word of God, as our authority from God for our understanding of all things that it addresses.[10] Part of the reason for this may lie in the fact that, though the Bible speaks on topics scientific, theological, historical, and literary, it doesn't fill in all of the details. Our heavenly Father may have left us to that task, to flesh out the skeletal outline, as it were, from our own investigations of science, history, ancient cultures, and archaeology. However, it does not seem to me that God, who is truth, who speaks truth, who reveals truth, can be trumped in

[10] We will investigate the scriptural testimony about the process by which Scripture came to be considered authoritative in chapter 2.

what He reveals by the limited understandings of men and women who, although we may do outstanding empirical research, are flawed and fallible.

In comparison to the God of creation and providence depicted in the Bible, who is omniscient, omnipotent, and omnipresent, our best efforts of understanding the unrevealed details (those left for our investigations outside the testimony of the Scriptures) are like the refrigerator art of our own children. Though we as parents may proudly display their work and derive pleasure from it, we still view it with a certain amount of humor.

Does the final authority rest in a perfect God, who revealed His truth in the words of the Bible, or in fallible man who fills in the details not revealed by the Bible? For nearly three thousand years, significant people groups have recognized the authority of the Judeo–Christian Scriptures as being the final word of divine revelation to man, both bearing truth and being truth from creator God on all things that He addresses.

No matter what one's denominational affiliation, all legitimate (i.e., non–cult) Christian churches base their belief systems, their dogma, their doctrine, on the words of the Bible. Some will add the authority of the church and its teachings in their thinking about authority, but even that thought is based in the pages of Scripture first (cf. Matt. 16:18–19).

Many of you reading this book are Christian leaders: pastors, para–church leaders, elders, deacons, administrators, and professors at Christian colleges and seminaries, Sunday school teachers, and home school parents/teachers. Allow me to ask you some questions for reflection. How many times in your teaching, instructing, admonishing, counseling, or directing others under your charge have you based your words and actions on the clear statements of Scripture?

How often, pastors, do you lead your elders or deacons in a Bible study on church organization and polity? No, no, this is not a guilt trip, as I am assuming that when you do so, you do so based in the words of Scripture. What is your rationale for doing so? Is it not that you really do regard the Scriptures as God's Word, and thus the authority you cite is His?

Christian school administrators, do you base your treatment of your faculty on the teaching in the pages of Scripture? I assume that you do, but why do you do it? Is it not because you also believe that the Bible and its teachings hold the authority of God, upon which you are able to make crucial decisions? I trust that you do.

Other evangelical leadership would normally be doing the same as they build their ministries, para–church organizations, and homeschools. They do so on the foundation of the Bible. Were the Bible not to reveal the truth of God to man in its pages, then what is the authority upon which any minister's work is built? Would it not be the shifting, sinking sands of a wanting foundation?

When I came to trust Jesus Christ as God's only provision for my sins at the age of nineteen, I did so in response to the proclamation of the Gospel from pulpits and in small group meetings at college. Had there not been a basic belief in the authority of the Bible as God's holy Word in those who shared these words, I doubt that I would have been swayed at all. I doubt that I would have been totally changed as I was. I doubt that I would have read the entire Bible within ten weeks of my conversion. I doubt that I would have begun publicly giving witness to my conversion by my wonderful Savior Jesus. If the Bible has no authority, or diminished authority, then having trusted Him, having been reborn, regenerated, forgiven, redeemed, and sealed by His Spirit (all truths of the Bible), all these would seemingly diminish in importance as well.

As evangelical leaders, then, it seems to me that we are faced with a choice. Either the entire Bible is our authority from God, or none of it is. Either we allow our culture to be our authority, or our "assured scientific conclusions" based on empirical observations to be that authority, or we return to the pages of Scripture for the authority granted to us by our God to proclaim truth in our increasingly secular society. We of all people must filter all that we perceive through the grid work of our Holy Book, the foundation and authority for the faith, and for the faithful of Christ.

Two: Revelation from God

Special Revelation

I begin the section on revelation from God as a whole by addressing what is called by many, *special revelation*. Whether it is the Word of God incarnate in the person of Christ, or the Word of God inscripturated in the pages of the Bible, special revelation from God is absolutely necessary for the Christian faith. Special revelation through the Bible is that which provides the historical account of the crucified, buried, and risen Jesus Christ, the foundation of our faith. We will therefore take a few moments to look at Scripture's testimony about itself and about the Savior. While this is not intended to be an exhaustive theology, it should suffice to reveal the necessary presuppositions that guide my thinking. After a few general details about the Bible, we will examine the Bible's self–testimony.

The Bible is an amazing book. For many, many years, it has outpaced all other books in sales. Basically, a quick look at the Bible reveals sixty-six different books; thirty-nine of which comprise the Old Testament, and twenty-seven the New Testament.[11] Chapter and verse divisions, which are not inspired, came many years after the *autographa* (the original writings).

Languages other than English will at times organize the sixty-six books in differing ways. For instance, the English Old Testament has four basic divisions: the Pentateuch, Historical Books, Poetical Books, and Prophetic Books. The Hebrew Bible contains three main parts: Torah, Nebi'im, and Kethubim. These three sections provide the acronym Tanakh for the entire corpus and stand for the Law, the Prophets, and the Writings

[11] Presupposition one: I hold neither the apocryphal nor pseudepigraphal books as canonical. However, I respect my Catholic friends who so regard the Apocrypha.

respectively. The final book of the Tanakh is not Malachi as in English versions. It is rather 2 Chronicles, thought to be the last book completed in ca. 380 BC.

The oldest translation of the Old Testament into another language is the Septuagint (abbreviated LXX), a Koine Greek version that dates from as early as 250 BC. An unusual feature of the LXX may be found in the book of Jeremiah, which is about 1/7 shorter than the Massoretic text of the Hebrew Bible (abbreviated as MT). Not only that, but many of the LXX chapters in Jeremiah are arranged differently than those of the MT or our English versions.

Traditional Christians of the past have believed that the Bible was written over a period of fourteen hundred years by about forty different authors, which is understood as the time of Moses through the apocalyptic writings of the Apostle John. Some would lengthen this amount of time for the Bible's development based in their belief that Job was the first book written shortly after the events of his life that are described therein (ca. 1800 BC). Others would instead shorten to about twelve hundred years depending on their view of a late date that the exodus occurred. Still some others would shorten it to about one thousand years total for both Old and New Testaments if they adhere to the Documentary hypothesis, popularized by Julius Wellhausen in 1878.[12]

---

[12] The Documentary hypothesis suggests that thorough literary analysis of the first five books of the Bible reveals a multi-authored work that was edited together over time, based in four source documents. These four documents are called the Jahwistic, dating from about 950 BC, the Elohistic dating from about 850 BC, the Deuteronomistic dating from about 622 BC, and the Priestly dating from about 450 BC (hence the well–known JEDP abbreviation for the hypothesis). Any of these dates would preclude Mosaic involvement, and though the basic premise of the Documentary hypothesis is unpopular with some, the derivatives of the Documentary hypothesis continue to garner the support of many, if not most, biblical scholars. This is despite the fact that many now no longer believe in the separate existence of E, and the dating of P has been called into question by the discovery of two silver amulets dating from roughly 650 BC at Keteph–Hinnom just outside of Jerusalem. These amulets record the paleo–Hebrew text of the great priestly blessing of Num. 6:24–26, previously held by most to be Priestly in origin (as is Gen. 1). Too, the work of Umberto Cassuto (*The Documentary Hypothesis*, Magnes Press, 1961), who maintained a belief in Mosaic authorship; and that of R. N. Whybray (*The Making of the Pentateuch*, JSOT Press, 1987), who did not; both have been effective in arguing against the major supporting arguments of the Documentary Hypothesis.

What does the Scripture say about itself? First of all, the Bible is a book of dual–authorship. By this I mean that God is behind the writing of each of the individual human authors. A straightforward reading of 2 Peter 1:20–21 says: "But know this first of all, that no prophecy of Scripture is a matter of one's own interpretation, for no prophecy was ever made by an act of human will, but men moved by the Holy Spirit spoke from God" (NASV).[13] One may say, strictly speaking, that this verse only refers to prophecy that was written down and later included in our canon of Scripture. The other viewpoint regards the phrase "prophecy of Scripture" as including both the foretelling and the forthtelling aspects of prophecy.[14] Either may be true, but the interpretation, whether broad to include all Scripture or narrow to include only the foretelling aspect of prophecy, still illustrates my point about the process of men who were borne along by the Holy Spirit who spoke from God. Somehow, the Spirit moved men to pen the words of God to us, but still retained the individual styles of those men who wrote. Then of course, one also finds 2 Timothy 3:16, which states: "All Scripture is inspired by God and is profitable for teaching, for reproof, for correction, for training in righteousness. . . ." The term used for "inspired" is *theopneustos*. This noun is composed of two Greek words, *theos* and *pneustos*, which are thought to yield a meaning of "God–breathed." Though one may maintain that only the prophetic parts of Scripture were involved in the type of divine activity described in 2 Peter 1:20–21, this verse in 2 Timothy 3:16 seems to indicate that at a minimum the Old Testament was God–breathed.[15] That of course would include Genesis 1–2.

---

[13] Unless otherwise noted, all NT quotes are taken from the *New American Standard Bible*.

[14] Thus reading an attributive genitive in the phrase, rather than a partitive genitive.

[15] Since St. Peter regarded the epistles of St. Paul to be included with what he called Scripture in 2 Peter 3:16 and since 2 Timothy was Paul's final epistle written near the end of his life, some view this verse to apply to at least some New Testament writings as well.

It is important to note what this verse does not mean. This verse does not mean that all of the Old Testament was verbally dictated by God, though that is certainly the case in some parts, such as perhaps sections in the Decalogue and some portions in Jeremiah. Otherwise, God revealed Himself at times in dreams and visions (through Joseph and Daniel for instance), through prophets moved by the Spirit, and through oracles, or burdens.[16]

In the minds of many, this process of inspiration by God's Spirit who moved men along as they wrote insured that the Scriptures were infallible and inerrant when first penned, i.e., in the original manuscripts, called the *autographa.*[17] Scripture supports the idea of an infallible text at several points. For instance, Jesus pointed out that every word of the Law, down to the smallest letter or even the smallest serif of a letter, would be fulfilled (Matt. 5:18). He also insisted on the veracity of verbal tenses of Exodus 3:6 ("I *am* the God of Abraham . . .") as He responded to the Pharisees in Matthew 22:32. Even Paul made a crucial theological point based in the singular form versus the plural as he quoted Genesis 22:17–18 in Galatians 3:16 ("He does not say 'and to seeds,' as *referring* to many, but *rather* to one, 'and to your seed,' that is, Christ"). Another reason that many evangelicals see the infallible nature of Scripture is found in the aside that Jesus offers in John 10:35 that the Scripture cannot be broken. Still others say that God who is true (Rom. 3:4; cf. John 14:6) would move men to write truthfully what He was breathing out. Psalm 119:160 affirms: "The sum of your word is truth."

---

[16] The process of dual authorship may be seen in Mark 12:36 which claims the Spirit's involvement when David wrote Psalm 110. The author of Hebrews is fond of ascribing the words of the Pentateuch to the Holy Spirit in Hebrews 3:7; cf. Hebrews 10:15–16.

[17] Even conservative evangelicals admit that the transmission of the Scripture over time by hand copying, though amazing and miraculous in preservation, was not inspired in the same way as were the *autographa.* The discipline, or study, of textual criticism helps us to determine the original reading, insofar as that is possible. Versions in the various languages come to life when this method has been applied.

Any discussion about the authority of the Bible as God's Word to man seems to go missing in today's understanding about the origins and age of the universe. One of the final words of Jesus before He ascended to the Father was: "All authority has been given to me in heaven and on earth" (Matt. 28:18). This is the same Jesus, the incarnated Word of God, which 1:14 of John's gospel reveals: "and the Word became flesh, and dwelt among us." It was through Him that all things came to be in the beginning (John 1:2–3). If these words have any rational meaning, they communicate that Jesus was the agent of the creative process in the beginning. Paul agrees: "For by Him all things were created, *both* in the heavens and on earth, visible and invisible, whether thrones or dominions or rulers or authorities—all things have been created by Him and for Him" (Col. 1:18). The incarnated Word, Jesus, having all authority over the heavens and the earth, which were created by Him and for Him, has given His inspired written Word to us so that we might learn about Him and come to know Him. For Him the Scripture is important on the utmost level because it is the inspired written Word of God from the incarnate Word of God, written through man, without error.

The words themselves are very important for mankind as well, holding authority over man because the ultimate author of those words holds authority over all things, including heaven and earth. Were it not for the Scriptures, we might believe that what we see in the created universe would be the final word, indeed the only word. Rather, it is the special revelation from God in the person of Christ and in the Bible that invests the created world with any revelatory value whatsoever. We call this value general revelation.

General Revelation

There is no doubt that the created universe is very important to the God who created it. In fact, the Bible says: "The heavens are recounting the glory of God, and the expanse is making known the work of His hands" (Ps. 19:1). Would we have that knowledge apart from God and His Word? It is doubtful. Rather we could conclude something entirely different. For some, a conclusion might be that there was a first cause somewhere; for others, a conclusion could be simply that all came into being by random chance.

This same created order does tell us as well something about the true God and man's responsibility to Him: "For since the creation of the world His invisible attributes, His eternal power and divine nature, have been clearly seen, being understood through what has been made, so that they are without excuse" (Rom. 1:20). But would we interpret the creation in that way were it not for the words of Paul in Romans? It is doubtful. Were it not for the special revelation of Scripture, it seems that man would not have come up with anything better than the pantheons of ancient cultures, which generally included gods made in the image of man. This is exactly what the ancient cultures such as Greece and Rome did.

Since it is the Scriptures from God that reveal that the created universe could have any revelatory value whatsoever, how is it that so many have elevated the observable created order (with its changing interpretations of empirical data) to sit as judge over the ancient written Word of God? There are *not* two Books of God, the one Book of Scripture and the one Book of Creation, both of equal value in declaring who God is and how the worlds came to be. The Bible does not even speak of a "Book of Creation," *per se*. If this were the case, one or the other must be preeminent. If the Scripture, given from the Word Incarnate, Jesus, through man, and thus inspired, infallible, and authoritative, is held as preeminent, then the created universe must take its place under the authority of God and His Scripture. Only by taking Scripture as preeminent can there be a possibility of harmony between special revelation and general revelation. If the created universe, the so–called "Book of Creation," is held preeminent, there can be no harmony. The Scripture will be ultimately relegated to the ash heap of history, and scientific interpretation of the created order will become god. More will be said later concerning the ramifications of allowing human interpretation of the creation's origin to sit as judge over God's revealed and authoritative Word in Genesis 1–2.

Three: Consistency in Hermeneutics

At a departmental luncheon held at the national meetings of the evangelical Theological Society about 2003, I interviewed my faculty colleagues from Bryan College's biblical studies division on the issue of the age of the earth as recorded in the Scriptures. Each of those good and godly men, only two of which now remain at the same school, all agreed that the issue was very important, but most did not have any definite defense of the biblical position at ready disposal. In other words, they were not prepared to offer an *apologia* for the young earth position, though all of them held to it. Obviously, each of those men was dependent on other scholars to study the issues and formulate biblically documentable positions. The problem is that too many Hebrew scholars have refused to do so, either to protect their own "academic credibility" or because they have not considered the ramifications that ignorance of the issues causes for the interpretation of Scripture as a whole. Because of this, a number of others who are less qualified have written books attempting to harmonize the Scriptures with their own understanding of science. Some biblical scholars have in turn been persuaded by the evidence presented and have abandoned any belief in the value of Genesis 1–2 as reflecting the origins of the heavens and the earth. This practice I see as crippling to the church at large, and helps to explain why the parishioner in the pew and the student in the classroom cry out for understanding. If our evangelical leaders do not answer the old earth position with a stalwart faith in the authority of the written Word of God, then what are we to believe? If the Bible is in error in Genesis 1–2 (or is simply etiological, allegorical, literary instead of literal, or purely metaphorical), wherein it does clearly state the method of creation (by the divine fiat of God) and the length of time it took (six twenty-four hour days), then why in the world should I believe that the Bible contains any truth at all? This dilemma I think is eroding the church at its very foundation, and must be reconciled if the church is to have any voice at all in this fallen and continually falling world.

The way of reconciliation about which I speak has many aspects. It is the way of consistency in hermeneutical practices. It is the way of evangelicals returning to a consistent faith position about the infallibility, inerrancy, and the authority of God's Word where it speaks not only to the issues of faith and practice but also to the issues of history and science. It is the way of godly men and women refusing to continue to bow down to human scientists who extrapolate data from empirical observations and interpret that data as inferring that our universe had little or no divine origin; or if it did, it did not happen the way the Bible testifies that it did. It is the way of godly men and women refusing to acquiesce to those evangelical leaders who name the name of Christ but have abandoned their own faith positions in Genesis 1–2 as part of the whole of authoritative Scripture in order to understand an old earth. It is the way of evangelical leaders who will refuse to yield to literary interpretations that divest Genesis 1–2 of any normal meaning, especially when such literary viewpoints are lacking in credible internal or external support.

Whether because they are well educated in other fields, or even in biblical studies, or whether they seek to "broaden the appeal" of their own public ministries, or whether they seek common ground for "evangelism," such individuals who avoid the issues of origins or purposefully move away from them actually do the church a grave disservice. You are our leaders, and our leaders are leading us away from the faith by means of the practice of allowing science to dictate our hermeneutical methods in Genesis 1–2. Can the virgin birth, vicarious substitutionary atonement, and resurrection be far-off?[18]

A great number of evangelical leaders with whom I speak, whether in church or in academia or in private conversations, simply avoid the issue of the age of the earth. Many have in fact simply thrown up their hands in despair at the discussion, which is in many ways clouded by sensory overload. For instance, the wonderful and awesome data pouring in from the Hubble telescope seems at first to be overwhelmingly insurmountable to any young earth position, given the presupposition of a consistency in the speed of light.[19] Too, the fossil record does indeed appear, at least at first look, to have been laid down over vast stretches of time, which would far exceed a few thousand years. Because of these and other marvelous discoveries in various scientific disciplines, many scholars and Christian leaders who choose to do so have attempted in numerous ways (some of which we will discuss below) to harmonize the words of Genesis 1–2 with an old earth position.

Any attempted harmonization with science on the issue of the age of the earth cannot be achieved if one wishes to be consistent in one's biblical *hermeneutic*, or, method of interpretation. Never in the history of the church of which I am aware, have so many allowed data from the scientific world to influence their thinking to the point that they are willing to undermine the clearly stated words of Scripture in an effort to be scholarly acceptable to their nonbelieving peers. This may ostensibly be done in an effort to achieve additional financial support in para–church ministries, greater academic recognition, or to build larger churches. Yet, no matter what the motivation, to achieve such acceptance they must be inconsistent in their hermeneutics. Now, they have the right to be inconsistent, certainly. I would not deny

---

[18] Tennessee District Attorney General (later US Senator) Thomas Stewart warned about this very possibility in the proceedings of the Scopes Trial in 1925.

[19] Again, I have heard that there is some evidence that the speed of light is actually slowing, but I don't know.

them this right. But they should also keep in mind that those who teach will receive a stricter judgment (James 3:1). One remembers that Job's friends were charged by an angry God in the wrongdoing of not speaking about Him that which was right (Job 42:7).

One cannot understand, believe, or teach any aspect of the Bible outside of Genesis 1 from any denominational perspective without engaging in a certain consistency of interpretation. The distinctions that separate denominations within Christianity usually focus on lexicographical, morphological, syntactical, and contextual nuances of the actual words of the Bible (and the theological developments of these issues over time). Rarely does the evangelical church turn to the scientific community on any other matters outside of the issue of the origins of the creation.

For instance, were I to study a passage concerning an aspect of the life of David, I might begin by reading the literary pericope in English several times to get the general flow, which enables one to sense the meta-narrative, i.e., the lesson that the passage is trying to communicate. Then I would study the passage in Hebrew, beginning first with a textual analysis so as to ascertain the original reading insofar as is possible. I would then study the individual words employing venerated lexicons, examining the basic meanings, etymologies, other occurrences of a given word in other contexts, and cognates. Next, I would attempt to understand the grammar (both the morphology and the phonology), as well as the syntactical nuances. I would want to discern the type of genre in which the passage is cast. I would want to understand the historical background, then the immediate context, and then I could move to comparative literatures of the ancient Near Eastern world, if necessary. Only as the very last resort would I move into an entirely differing discipline to seek a definitive interpretation, and that only if earlier results had been unclear. Notice that I did not say here "only if earlier results were not acceptable in the discipline that I finally appealed to." To make my point perfectly clear to my reader, I would never eschew the clear words of Scripture from God Almighty so I could be academically acceptable to the scientific community or to the community of Christians who follow that scientific community so closely.

Let me offer a brief test study of an important passage. Were you and I to go to Matthew 1:18–25 and there read the account of the virgin birth of Jesus of Nazareth (as countless millions of Christians have done for nearly two thousand years), what should we conclude? The words are clear and the passage well written. This passage has been interpreted consistently throughout generations as one of the foundational building blocks of the church's belief system. That Jesus was born unlike any man in all of creation or history is a fundamental to the faith. He was born by a virgin. However, science tells us that virgin birth among humans, *parthenogenesis*, is an impossibility, or that if it were to occur by chance, the infant would be female.[20] That being the case, evangelical leaders who wish to be consistent with interpretation must either believe the clear words of Scripture, or the findings of science. There is no other rational understanding of the Koine Greek term *parthenos* in biblical contexts than that of a virgin. There is no other reasonable explanation to the word "born." There is no harmonization here. The only reason there would ever be to attempt harmonization would be if the scientific community were to attempt to make it an issue in the public school system. But there is no reason to do that really, is there? The

[20] This latter understanding of the gender of a child resulting from *parthenogenesis*, were it ever to actually happen, is recounted from my memory. In this case, I will leave documentation to someone else!

damage really has been done already by assaulting the early chapters of Genesis, which are foundational to every other doctrine in Scripture.[21]

Admittedly, the scriptural position concerning the virgin birth of Christ is a matter of faith. It is also vitally important to several cardinal tenets of the faith, such as the hypostatic union of Christ,[22] the sinlessness of Christ, and the substitutionary atonement of Christ (2 Cor. 5:21, 1 Pet. 3:18). Yet, we can believe the Scripture that Jesus was born of a virgin, a fact consistent either as the antitype of Isaiah 7:14 or as its prophetic fulfillment, and still agree with science that this is not normally the case in *homo sapiens*. It did happen once. That's why it is called a miracle. It differs from what we normally expect to happen.

Were I to go to Luke 24:5b–6a and read there (as countless millions of Christians also have done for nearly two thousand years): "Why do you seek the living among the dead? He is not here, but He has risen" (NASV), what process of interpretation should I use? Using my basic procedural outline above, I would probably conclude at the end of my study that Jesus, once dead, is alive. Other Scripture convinces me (as it has laypeople and scholars who have translated our Bibles from the original languages of Hebrew, Aramaic, and Koine Greek) that He is still living today. However, science states categorically that when the human body dies, it stays that way. There is no coming back. There is no resurrection in the sense of never dying again (though those resuscitated will die again, as with Lazarus in the Bible and others who have had near-death experiences). evangelical pastors, professors, and leaders of para–church organizations normally approach this passage from a faith position. Even though they may have abandoned the young earth position for an old earth position

[21] The serpent did this as early as Genesis 3:4 when he categorically contradicted God's Word.
[22] Jesus of Nazareth is fully God and fully man in one person, giving rise to the term "hypostatic union."

because of the pervasiveness of acceptance of Darwinian evolution or its religious alternative (theistic evolution), they would never consider abandoning their belief in the resurrection of Jesus Christ just because science says it's impossible. My question to them is: Why should you bow to science in the question of the origins of the earth yet refuse to bow to them in the question of the possibility of resurrection?" To which one may reply, "Because the resurrection is historical fact, supported by numerous biblical passages, historical traditions, and the existence of the church throughout the centuries. The question of origins is debatable." To this I would reply: "Why is the question of origins, for you who so strongly believe in the resurrection of Christ, debatable? Genesis 1–2 are also offered as historical fact, supported by numerous biblical passages, historical traditions, and supported by this same Church throughout the centuries." My opponent could reply: "but the evidence of an old earth is overwhelming." By so stating, my debate opponent has bowed the knee to science. Science has just mastered his thinking, taken its seat, and become judge over Scripture.

There can be no harmonization in the pages of Scripture with old earth interpretations derived from scientific inquiry. Are there any points of agreement? Sure. We as believers in Christ can agree with science that the earth does seem to be quite old. We disagree on how the fossil record came to be, particularly that this record seems to indicate great antiquity. We can agree that our present understanding of starlight travel time presents a very difficult contrast to the young earth position. This alone would cause the present author to leave a young earth position, were it not for the fact that I hold the Bible as preeminent and authoritative in all that it teaches, not just in faith and practice but also where it speaks in areas normally investigated by scientists and mathematicians. Once again, it is absolutely not that I denigrate science or scientific inquiry. Not at all. It is that I disagree with some of science's interpretations of the data where it clearly contradicts Scripture, since I hold the Bible to be preeminent and authoritative. It, not science, is the final Word on the subject.

For all evangelicals, science should indeed be held in high regard, in high esteem. It has been scientific investigation that has led to the discovery of electricity, the development of the lightbulb, the telephone, the cell phone, the computer. It has been scientific hypotheses, experimentations, and theories that have led to space exploration, to a better understanding of the universe in which we live. Scientific experimentation has led to better health, to vaccines to protect from rabies, from polio, from smallpox; science has helped us to control diabetes, to slow the growth of cancerous tumors. Scientific experimentation allows us to better understand weather patterns, crop production, and the effects of pesticides. The lists of laudable scientific accomplishments continue to grow daily.[23] We should applaud the daily efforts and the lifetime achievements of the men and women who work honestly and diligently in the pursuit of better scientific observation, inquiry, theory, and practical applications for the betterment of mankind.

All of these wonders of science and scientists may be lauded, but for evangelicals who wish to honor the authority that is God's Word, these achievements must be understood as simply the results of the investigation of God's created order. Scripture is the starting point, from which science should begin its inquiry.[24] When science begins to take empirical data and extrapolate that which is now back into that which once was to the point of denying the Bible's teaching on a given subject, then there is a problem. In other words, when science begins to deny the Creator His biblically crucial position as Creator, there is a problem. Or,

---

[23] On the other hand, science has also given us biological and chemical agents, and atomic capabilities that could eradicate us.

[24] In fact, theology was once lauded as the "queen of the sciences."

when science begins to deny the method that God created, there is a problem. Or, when science begins to deny the clear teaching of the length of time it took for the creation to be, there is a problem. And where there is a problem, evangelicals face a choice much like ancient Israel did on Mt. Carmel many centuries ago. The prophet Elijah challenged the gathered peoples: "If Baal be god, then serve him; but if YHWH be God, serve Him." I challenge evangelicals today: "If science be God on the matters of the origins of the universe, then serve science; but if the God of the Bible be the Creator, then serve Him."

Numerous times those who believe in a young earth based solely in the authority of the simple reading of Genesis are mocked as "flat–earthers." Though there still exists today a society bearing that name, with individuals who believe that the earth is flat, young earthers are very rarely a part of them.[25] Nothing in Scriptures clearly indicates that the earth is flat. Earlier appeals to the expression "four corners of the earth" (Isaiah 11:12; Rev. 7:1) for conclusive evidence of a flat earth have subsequently been found lacking. The phrase has been found to be an ancient Near Eastern idiom for the four directions of the compass. On the other hand, the Scriptures are abundantly clear about the recent creation offered in Genesis 1–2, supported by the text itself, as we shall see below. The only time, the only way, the words of Genesis 1–2 are not clear is when we allow scientific conclusions to take priority over the authoritative Word of God. Only when science becomes God is the issue obfuscated. We now turn our attention to the self–revelation of the Bible's God in the clear words and structures of Genesis 1.[26]

---

[25] There are still a few who hold to geocentrism, that is, that the universe revolves around the earth. I regard this position as untenable.

[26] Presupposition two: I take the Bible as the inspired, inerrant, infallible, and authoritative Word of God to man that gives meaning both to His incarnate Word and to the created universe. Therefore, my study will emphasize the individual words of Genesis 1 and 2, which I hold as unchanging, rather than the findings of science, which seem to be changing regularly. For instance, some believe that many if not most of the

arguments used as evidence for evolutionary theory in the Scopes Monkey Trial of 1925 have been subsequently shown to be erroneous at best, hoaxes at worst. However, other than a few minor changes due to versional differences and minor transmission errors, the Bible is the same now as it has been for nearly two thousand years.

Four: The Genre of Genesis 1

The interpretation of Genesis 1:1–2:3 has long been a matter of interest to many expositors of the Scriptures. Of particular interest has been the length of time involved in the creation. Though the Hebrew text seems to indicate this length in terms of six earth "days" of twenty-four hours each, further defined by the terms "evening" and "morning," many have seen lengthier periods of time indicated in those same terms. The Patristic writers, for instance, seem to be mixed in their understanding of the passage, even though the tradition of six twenty-four- hour days goes back at least as far as the Priestly writer, or in my thinking, to Moses himself: "For six days the Lord made the heavens and the earth and the sea and all which is in them, and He rested on the seventh day" (Ex. 20:11).

In the last two hundred years, the developments in source criticism, comparative Semitic literature and language, and genre studies, coupled with Darwinism and its aftermath, have greatly intensified the discussion among evangelicals. Many have abandoned the recent, quick creation viewpoint, opting instead for one that suggests that the terms used to express time passage in Genesis 1:1–2:3 are to be understood symbolically or metaphorically, as figures of speech instead of six sequential twenty-four–hour days. Such attempts fail to be conclusive or even plausible in the light of genre analysis, as will be seen below.

Some justify this change of understanding in Genesis 1 based on their perception of the way that the term "day" (*yôm*) is used in Scripture. Hugh Ross, a popular spokesperson for the progressive creationist viewpoint, claims that *yôm* is broad enough to include a meaning of millions or billions of years.[27] Others would call it a metaphor for a lengthy period of time, an "anthropomorphic" day so to speak. This they understand simply as a term used for the benefit of humans who cannot comprehend the time needed for the Creative process.[28] Some others would refer to it as a day of God's revelation to Moses, though such a concept is foreign to the context of the passage.[29]

In order to justify these interpretations that abandon a literal twenty-four-hour day, commentators must, consciously or not, deal with the concept of literary genre.[30] It is the purpose of this chapter generally to engage the discussion of the genre of the creation account as it informs our understanding of the details of the passage. In other words, differing types of literature may allow for differing ways of interpreting similar data. Waltke has recently noted: "In light of the biblical text's literary genre, the reader will be in a better position to decide the compatibility or the incompatibility of this creation account with scientific theories of origin."[31] Did you catch this? Waltke says that proper understanding of the genre of the passage is paramount in the issue of whether or not the Genesis creation account is compatible with scientific theories of origin! It is with this in mind that we now engage this issue of genre.

There are only three major choices of genre of Scripture available to use when interpreting Genesis 1:1–2:3: prophecy, poetry, or narrative (with several subcategories of each to consider). This essay will first investigate which of these three broad categories fits the Genesis account of creation, then attempt to analyze which if any subcategory best fits.

---

[27] Hugh Ross, *Creation and Time*, (NavPress, 1994), 11, 45–52.

[28] C. John Collins, "How Old Is the Earth? Anthropomorphic Days in Genesis 1:1–2:3," *Presbyterion* 20/2 (1994), 117.

[29] Duane Garrett, *Rethinking Genesis*, (Mentor, Geanies House, Ross–shire, Great Britain, 2000), 193.

[30] Genre may be defined as a readily identifiable type of literature, such as prose versus. poetry, or an encyclopedia article versus. a text message.

[31] Bruce K. Waltke, "The Literary Genre of Genesis, Chapter 1," *Crux* 27:4 (1991), 2.

Following this examination, we will consider a special creation genre suggested by some, built at least in part on the framework hypothesis.[32]

Genesis 1:1–2:3 as Prophecy

Some advocate understanding the Genesis account of creation as prophecy.[33] This is done ostensibly by claiming that the few morphologically ambiguous verbal forms are to be interpreted as specific future imperfects ("the waters will teem with fish") rather than jussives of command ("let the waters teem with fish"). Unfortunately for this hypothesis, Hebrew grammar will allow this interpretation only for the verb forms used only on days 5 and 6, with the creation of animals of the seas, heavens and land, inasmuch as the verb forms used on days 1–4 are uniquely identified as jussives by their *morphology* (form). Too, the same daily pattern (of command, fulfillment, assessment, and equal time) that is used for days 5 and 6 is also used for days 1–4.[34] That pattern seems to demand that all of the verb forms be read the same way — in other words, that the ambiguous forms are to be read as jussives of command, like the unambiguous verb forms of the remainder of the passage.[35] The burden of proof falls on those who would argue differently.

Too, if prophetic, the passage does not fit into any of the understood prophetic sub–genres. These include salvation oracles, damnation oracles, exhortations, covenant lawsuits, disputations, and apocalyptic literature. Each of these are identifiable by content, structure, vocabulary, and at times, figures of speech employed. The Genesis account of creation does

---

[32] A fuller discussion of the Framework hypothesis and its implications is found in appendix A.

[33] Though I have not personally observed such a position in print, I have heard such proclamations on various radio programs dealing with the issue of creation versus evolution. Usually, these pronouncements are made by persons untrained in biblical studies.

[34] Bill T Arnold, *Encountering the Book of Genesis*, (Baker, 1998), 23; Bruce K . Waltke, *Genesis: a Commentary*, (Zondervan, 2001), 56.

[35] A further development as to why these verbal forms cannot be specific future imperfects is found in chapter 6.

not fit into any of these subcategories, so Genesis 1:1–2:3 absolutely cannot be considered prophetic.

Genesis 1:1–2:3 as Poetry

One of the more common ways to deal with Genesis 1:1–2:3 is to regard it as poetry, a literary work. This viewpoint thus opens the possibility for a nonliteral understanding of the words it employs. Some of the finest expositors of the passage have noted its elevated style, yet fall short of categorically naming it as poetry. Umberto Cassuto has said:

> . . . in the course of the biblical story, which is mainly in prose, the special importance of the subject led to an exaltation of style approaching the level of poetry, the thought took on of its own accord, as it were, an aspect conforming to the traditional pattern of narrative poetry—an aspect, at all events, that was in keeping with ancient poetic tradition.[36]

Bill Arnold has said: "Its elevated style is more like poetry and the unit is unique when compared to the narrative sections you will read elsewhere in Genesis." [37]

Indeed, much has been made of the symmetry involved between days 1–3 and days 4–6 in the passage;[38] about the cycle of introduction, command, report, evaluation, and time sequence of each diurnal activity;[39] about the repetition of key phrases;[40] and even about the numerical symbolism present.[41] However, style and structure alone are not determinative to designate a biblical Hebrew passage as poetic, as we will see below. Its "exalted style" could just as easily be the work of a narrator who is also a skilled writer, inspired by an infinite God to express the beauty of creation in a most beautiful way. For instance, there are also

---

[36] Umberto Cassuto, *A Commentary on the Book of Genesis: Part One: From Adam to Noah*, (Magnes Press, Jerusalem, 1961), 11.
[37] Arnold, *Encountering the Book of Genesis*, 23.
[38] Allen Ross, *Creation and Blessing*, (Baker, 1988), 104.
[39] Arnold, *Encountering the Book of Genesis*, 23.
[40] Repetition is actually a key component of historical narrative (John Sailhamer, *The Pentateuch as Narrative*, (Zondervan, 1992), 25).
[41] Cassuto, 12–19.

observable patterns of symmetry, style, and structure in the book of Acts, yet no one maintains that it is poetry.[42]

Genesis 1:1–2:3 as a whole is not Hebrew poetry, and there are many problems for those who would see it as such. Overall, it does not contain the most important and determinative structural feature of Hebrew poetry: balance between juxtaposed lines. This is commonly known as parallelism, which may be illustrated quickly by Psalm 119:105: "Your word is a lamp for my feet, and a light for my path."

A secondary characteristic of biblical Hebrew poetry is metrical balance within lines of poetry. Metrical balance involves the number of syllables counted within each part of a line, called a colon (plural: cola). Two cola comprise a line of poetry, typically having a syllable count of 4:4; 4:5; 5:5; 5:6, or the like. Two lines then form a couplet. In the case of Genesis 1:1–2:3 this type of metrical balance seems to exist only in 1:27, not throughout the entire section. So though 1:27 may be considered biblical Hebrew poetry on this metrical basis (and that is still debatable), the entire passage is not.

There are admittedly a number of figures of speech (which is a characteristic normally associated with biblical Hebrew poetry) in the initial section of 1:1–2:3,[43] but not in an inordinate amount for normal Hebrew prose. For instance, if the construction "God said" is indeed to be understood as an anthropomorphic figure of speech, and if the presence of such figures of speech automatically mandates a passage to be in the poetic genre, then a myriad of passages within the Pentateuch's historical narratives would have to be re-categorized as poetry. The implication of this would be that every time the Scripture says

[42] Consider that the structure of the book follows the pattern established in Acts 1:8: the disciples were to be witnesses for Christ in Jerusalem (chs. 1–7), in Judea and Samaria (chs. 8–12), and to the remotest parts of the earth (chs. 13–28). Many believe that Revelation 1:19 serves a similar function for that apocalyptic book.

[43] Merism in 1:1 and perhaps in 1:2 with *tōhû wābōhû*; perhaps anthropomorphism in the phrase "God said" in 1:3, 1:6, 1:9, 1:11.

"God said" we would have to understand that particular passage as being figurative rather than literal! Such an idea, particularly in contexts where God is revealing the stipulations of covenant obedience by His people, is preposterous! The point here is that the presence of figures of speech alone is not determinative of genre, inasmuch as figures of speech are found in all three major genres of Scripture: in narrative, prophecy, and poetry. The fact remains that the determinative structural indicator for Hebrew poetry is parallelism, which does not occur anywhere in the initial pericope other than perhaps in 1:27.

Anyone familiar with the work of Bernard Anderson or Claus Westermann has been exposed to the various genres of poetic literature, especially as applied in the Psalter.[44] Such genres include individual and communal laments, declarative and descriptive praises, pilgrim psalms, wisdom psalms, royal psalms, enthronement psalms, hallel psalms, songs of ascent, and the songs of Zion. Each of these can be identified by certain structural and/or rhetorical devices in the case of laments, praises, and wisdom psalms; or by groupings, as in the case of the Hallel (Pss. 113–18) or the Songs of Ascent (Pss. 120–34). Though there may be disagreement from time to time over how to classify a given psalm, most would agree that these are the available sub-categories of the genre of Hebrew poetry.

In content, the closest that Genesis 1:1–2:3 comes to any of the poetic genres is to that of a praise psalm. Praise psalms may be of two types: declarative praises and descriptive praises. Genesis 1:1–2:3 cannot be a declarative praise psalm, for that sub-genre would normally reveal what God has done for the individual or the nation, and which would normally be offered in the first person voice of the person or group delivered. Nor can it be a descriptive praise hymn, as these hymns depict the attributes of God in the fixed format of a

[44] Bernhard W. Anderson, *Out of the Depths*, Westminster, Philadelphia, 1983; Claus Westermann, *Praise and Lament in the Psalms*, John Knox, 1981.

call to praise, followed by a cause for praise, followed in turn by a renewed call or vow of praise. So the passage, though certainly revealing God as an all–powerful Creator, does not fit the sub-genre of a descriptive praise psalm.

Not only does Genesis 1:1–2:3 not fit into known poetic genres, it contrasts with creation passages that are in the poetic genre, such as the wisdom discourse of Proverbs 8:22–31 or the creation-based account of Job 38–41. And since Genesis 1 does not contain the parallelism or metrical balance necessary for the broad category designation of poetry; how then can it be considered as poetry at all? It is therefore amazing to me, inasmuch as it is clearly not Hebrew poetry, that the editors of the NIV have opted to format 1:1–2:3 as indented text, reminiscent of poetic verse.[45] What is perhaps even more surprising is that many are quick to name it as poetry without even considering the criteria which are crucial to identify biblical Hebrew poetry.

It is perhaps even more startling that so many want to interpret the individual words of Genesis 1:1–2:3 as symbolically as if they were in poetic genre. Those who would do so choose to ignore the normally understood criteria for interpreting a passage under the rubric of Hebrew poetry. Genesis 1:1–2:3 is not Hebrew poetry and individual words are not necessarily to be understood symbolically.

Genesis 1:1–2:3 as Narrative Prose

Most have seen the creation account as narrative, though into which subcategory of narrative it falls is widely debated. Until recently, this debate perhaps has been exacerbated by discordant definitions. John Sailhamer, for instance, sees the passage as a clear example

[45] I am aware of only one Hebrew manuscript that indents the narrative Genesis passage in the manner that the *Biblia Hebraica Stuttgartensia* does its poetical books. All other Hebrew manuscripts format it as narrative. The NIV remains the sole English version that indents as poetic.

of historical narrative.[46] Edward Young sees it as "a factual account of what actually occurred."[47] Van Wolde calls it a narrative story, [48] and Schottroff entitles her feminist work "The Creation Narrative: Genesis 1.1–2.4a."[49] Sternberg, while affirming the passage as narrative, qualifies it as an asymmetrical demonstration of God's omnipotence, i.e., "wherever God works wonders unseen by humanity."[50] Ostensibly, this feature would distinguish it from subsequent narratives of the symmetrical kind, those observable by humanity. After stating the passage is narrative, Brueggemann espouses that it is neither history nor myth.[51] Nahum Sarna affirms it as non-mythological narrative.[52] Claus Westermann designates the section as narrative, but sees the description as needing modification.[53] He maintains that it differs from the subcategory of narrative called story in that there is no tension to be resolved. Instead, the "narrative of Gen 1 is characterized by its onward, irresistible and majestic flow that distinguishes it so clearly from the drama narrated in Gen 2–3."[54] Westermann concludes that it "has acquired this peculiar narrative form which is really no narrative at all."[55]

---

[46] Sailhamer, 25.

[47] Edward J. Young, *Studies in Genesis 1*, An International Library of Philosophy and Theology: Biblical and Theological Studies, ed. J. Marcellus Kik, (Presbyterian and Reformed, 1976), 1.

[48] E. J. Van Wolde, "The Text as an Eloquent Guide: Rhetorical, Linguistic and Literary Features in Genesis 1," in *Literary Structure and Rhetorical Strategies in the Hebrew Bible*, (Eisenbraun's, 1996), 134.

[49] Luise Schottroff, "The Creation Narrative: Genesis 1.1–2.4a," in *A Feminist Companion to Genesis*, 1993, 24–38.

[50] Meir Sternberg, *The Poetics of Biblical Narrative*, (Indiana U. Press, 1985), 125.

[51] Walter Brueggemann, *Genesis*, Interpretation, (John Knox Press, 1973), 8, 16.

[52] Nahum Sarna, *Understanding Genesis*, (Schocken Books, 1970), 9.

[53] Westermann, *Genesis 1–11*, 80.

[54] Ibid.

[55] Ibid.

Fortunately, the recent work by George Coats provides a convenient nomenclature for classifying the sub–genres of narrative. [56] Possible major categories would be Tale, Legend, History, Report, Fable, Etiology, and Myth. Some of these may be excluded immediately, because Genesis 1:1–2:3 does not fit the basic literary criteria needed for such identification. In other words, Genesis does not contain the Hebrew equivalent of our "once upon a time," which commonly indicates a fairy tale, nor the final "and the moral of this story is . . ." of a fable. Too, some of these choices are not theologically palatable to evangelicals. For instance, we would not accept the categories of tales, legends, fables, and myths in Scripture insofar as those categories are commonly understood as containing statements that are clearly contrary to fact.[57] At the same time, many evangelical interpreters would accept the possibility of a bit of mytho–poetic language employed as a polemic within poetic or prophetic literature. After all, Israel's literature often reflected on aspects of pagan culture. On the other hand, history, report, and etiology are easier to accept as possibilities, since these ostensibly may involve the truth. For instance, Coats states that "History as a genre of literature represents that kind of writing designed to record the events of the past as they actually occurred."[58]

To this short list of possible truth–bearing narrative genres, one might be able to add the subcategories legal material (as the book of the covenant in Ex 20–24; or the book of Lev), covenant/treaty formula (such as the book of Deut), royal inscription (recounting the glories of a given king, such as Solomon in 1 Kgs 4:21–5:18), and succession narratives (a narrative that recounts how a king receives power from his predecessor and employs it to

---

[56] George W. Coats, *Genesis, with an Introduction to Narrative Literature*, vol. 1 of Rolf Knierim and Gene M. Tucker, eds., Forms of the Old Testament Literature, (Eerdman's, 1983), 5–10.

[57] The issue of the authority of Scripture as revelation given from God, and therefore revealed truth, is an essential part of evangelicalism.

[58] Coats, 9.

expand his kingdom, such as the story of David's kingship in 2 Sam). One can quickly see that Genesis 1:1–2:3 does not fit into any of these final four. Therefore, the only recognized and documentable genre possibilities for the narrative Genesis account of creation are history, report, and etiology.

Of these three (history, report, and etiology), many would say that the passage should be understood as historical narrative. This is because a report is seen as a simple, true account, and an etiology is normally a single line of writing, understood to be recounting a past event which explains a present circumstance. Genesis 1:1–2:3 fits the pattern of neither of these because it is neither simple nor short. Rather, John Sailhamer says that it is "clearly recognizable as a unit of historical narrative. It has an introduction (1:1), a body (1:2–2:3), and a conclusion (2:3). These three segments form a unit."[59] Other structural indicators of historical narrative that Sailhamer indicates are "sequence, disjuncture, repetition, deletion, description, and dialogue."[60] Genesis 1:1–2:3 has the sequence of the order of days, it has disjuncture at 1:2, repetition in the phrases "and it was so," "and it was good," "there was evening and there was morning," "the xth day,"[61] and so on. While lacking dialogue between humans, it does have dialogue of God with the creation and God with Himself (1:26). When one adds to the repetition (throughout the Gen 1 account) of the typical narrative diagnostic indicator *wayyiqṭōl* (verbs prefixed with *waws* consecutive or conversive, if one prefers),[62] then it becomes reasonably clear that the genre of the passage was intended to fall within the category of historical narrative.

---

[59] Sailhamer, 25.

[60] Ibid.

[61] "xth" day represents first day, second day, third day, fourth day and so on when describing the sequences in Gen. 1.

[62] Narrative sequencing of the past in biblical Hebrew is often commenced with a perfect tense verb followed by a series of preterite forms (basic imperfect for the strong verb or shortened imperfect for some weak verbs, prefixed by the *wāw* consecutive). Such is the case in 1:1–2:3.

Is it possible for Genesis 1:1–2:3 to be historical narrative and still contain figures of speech? After all, figures of speech have been claimed for this passage.[63] Although figures of speech are more abundant in poetic literature, they are not uncommon in other historical narratives. For instance, God uses both simile and literary hyperbole when He informs Abraham that his descendants will be like the stars of heaven or like the sand on the seashore in number (Genesis 15:5; 22:17).[64] We are informed again by simile that in Solomon's time, silver was like stones in Jerusalem (1 Kings 10:27). Other types of figures that may be seen in narrative include euphemism, which is using socially acceptable language for unpleasant topics ("pass away" instead of "die") and anthropomorphism ("the eye of the Lord is on those who fear Him"). At times, these figures are easily identifiable. At other times they may be illumined by comparative Semitic studies, such as in the case of Deuteronomy 11:10 where "to water with the foot" could be an idiom from Egypt where irrigation canals had sluice gates that were operated by the use of the foot. Another example may be numerical hyperbole in Scripture, recognized only because of its abundant attestation in royal inscriptions of the nations of the Semitic world. Figures of speech seem to be rather common in narratives in both Scripture and ancient Near Eastern (ANE) literature. Thus, of all the known literature of the ancient Near East, Genesis 1:1–2:3 best fits the genre historical narrative. The passage fits no other known genre.

Genesis 1:1–2:3 as a Special Creation Genre

[63] For instance, a merism, stating two extremes which include everything between, occurs in 1:1: "the heavens and the earth." There may also be merism involved in the terms "formless and void" in 1:2, meaning total disorder. Anthropomorphism may be seen in the phrase "and God said," though with the emphasis in Scripture on creation being by means of the divine word (cf. Ps 33:8–9, John 1:1–5, Heb 11:3) some could argue that He actually did speak and thus this should not be seen as anthropomorphism (Young, 55–58).

[64] Similes are comparisons that employ the terms "like" or "as." Literary hyperbole is seen in comparing Abraham's offspring to the countless number of the grains of sand.

Recently, some are claiming for Genesis 1:1–2:3 what essentially amounts to a separate category of genre that has no ANE parallel.[65] In his 1991 *Crux* article and again in his commentary on Genesis in 2001, Bruce Waltke, following Henri Blocher, claims for the creation account a genre more described than named: "a literary–artistic representation of the creation."[66] It is to be seen in this view as comprising elements of both historical narrative and metaphorical poetry. As such, it is narrative in form, but uses the most significant words in a manner uniquely distinct from their usage elsewhere in the Bible. The flexibility that comes with arbitrarily attaching any meaning one wishes to any word in the text allows one to have the text say anything one wishes. It could, for example, be used to mesh the biblical text with any theory of science of choice. As such, it could affirm that God is the Creator of all things, but instead of creation being the immediate response to the divine command issued over six successive literal twenty-four-hour days, the narrative could intend no implications at all regarding the time issue. The passage then may still be seen as a polemic against the other ANE gods, and it may still serve as a model for the human workweek and Shabbat (Sabbath), since God did it all in six anthropomorphic "God days," but we may no longer understand it to be communicating a relatively recent nor quick creation. But is this proposal likely?

It may be said here that Genesis 1:1–2:3 is indeed unique in both the Bible and in the milieu of the ANE.[67] No other passage dealing with the creation in the OT comes close to the style or structure of the Genesis account (other passages, as Job 38–41, Pss. 8, 74, 104, and Proverbs 8 are all clearly poetic in genre). As compared with the ANE cosmogonies, the

[65] This may be called a biblical cosmology, an older term now to be imbued with new meaning. Or, it may yet be called the "special creation Genre." Cf. Waltke, "The Literary Genre," 9.
[66] Waltke, "The Literary Genre," 9; *Genesis 1–11*, 78.
[67] John H. Walton, *Ancient Israelite Literature in its Cultural Context*, (Regency/Zondervan, 1989), 34.

Genesis account differs in several ways: creation is by divine decree; creation is offered within a time framework of six days; no struggle is evident (i.e., it is not a dualistic cosmogony); the purpose of man is not an afterthought but the pinnacle of the narrative, etc.[68]

It is my contention that even if the Genesis creation account is to be taken as a special and unique creation genre, then we as biblical scholars are constrained by normal hermeneutics to interpret the passage as well as we can within parameters established by the literature of the Bible and comparative ANE documents. This means avoiding the temptation to yield too quickly to the evolving conclusions of science. This means trying to answer the questions that arise in a manner intra–contextually, intra–biblically, and intra–culturally before we interact with extra-biblical scientific findings.[69] And at present, it must be analyzed within the genre it best fits, namely, the genre of historical narrative.

Genre identification, though not absolutely determinative in every case for the purposes of interpretation, can be extremely helpful if a particular conundrum arises. For instance, in my doctoral dissertation, I found that biblical historical literature that included enormous numbers often paralleled other ancient Near Eastern literature. In similar ANE royal inscriptions, large numbers were often employed to glorify a given king. This in turn helped to understand the reason such large numbers were employed in Scripture: they glorify the King of Kings. Therefore, the largest numbers of Scripture, found in biblical literature of

---

68 Gerhard F. Hasel, "The Significance of the Cosmology of Genesis 1 in Relation to Ancient Near Eastern Parallels," *Andrews University Seminary Studies* 10 (1972): 1–20.

69 As an example, one might take the word "fish" in Hebrew, which is *dag*. One would study the lexicography of the root word to obtain the gloss "fish" to begin with. Then one would study the word in its various contexts to ascertain its semantic field, which might yield a spectrum of meanings of differing types and sizes of fish. Next one might study the various syntactical structures in which the word occurs to determine if there are any nuances to be considered. Then one might study cognate words in other cultures. Finally, one might consult science for biological terminology. It is doubtful, however, except perhaps in the case of myth or fantasy, that the word "fish" would ever mean "aardvark."

the same or similar genre to the royal inscriptions of the ANE, may be interpreted as numerical hyperbole.[70] By analogy, might the same thing be happening with the term "day" and the phrase "and there was evening and there was morning" in Genesis 1:1–2:3? (These are, of course, the terms that give rise to the impetus to seek another genre.) This is at least a possibility, but there is as yet no other ANE literature comparable to the Genesis account of creation with which to compare. To state that the Genesis account is a differing genre seems to be an arbitrary choice by those who do not wish to see it as literal historical narrative with its accompanying implications of time passage. To simply declare it to be a different genre without any other similar examples anywhere in the ANE world is untenable and appears to be special pleading.

In recent publications concerning Genesis 1:1–2:3, the discussions have centered primarily on the use of "day" (*yôm*). As I hope it will be clearly demonstrated in my discussion in chapter 6, "day" and "days" are never used elsewhere in the Hebrew Bible in the sense of multiple thousands or millions of years, i.e., the period of time necessary for evolution to have occurred. The burden of proof rests upon those who would argue differently. Of course, my conclusions were based on understanding Genesis 1:1–2:3 as historical narrative. It is precisely at this point that others may wish to see the Genesis creation account as an entirely separate genre: the normally understood biblical usage of *yôm* seems inadequate to account for the information available to us from empirical analysis of the cosmos in which we live. If the passage is a different genre, perhaps we can understand *yôm* as representing millions of years, accepting in the term what some have deemed to be "anthropomorphic" days. That is, "day" is not meant to be a humanly perceived day of

[70] David M. Fouts, "A Defense of the Hyperbolic Interpretation of Large Numbers in Old Testament," *Journal of the Evangelical Theological Society* 40 (1997): 377–87.

twenty-four-hours duration, but an indefinite time period. Were this to be the case, God would in Genesis 1 be condescending to mankind's very limited understanding. The choice of "day" then becomes only usable in support of the six–day workweek capstoned by Shabbat (Gen. 2:2–3; Exod. 20:11), not for any valid measurement of time length of creation. This suggestion will be shown to be untenable in the discussions below.

If Genesis 1:1–2:3 is a special genre with certain words having unique meanings (and it has yet to be established that it does, since it best fits known genres under the rubric of historical narrative), then those words will have different meanings in Genesis 1:1–2:3 than in historical narrative. To justify a unique meaning for a word in the creation account, one must search outside biblical historical narrative for that justification. Yet, when it is argued, for example, that *yôm* does occasionally mean an indefinite period of time, this appeal is generally made to occurrences of the word in historical narrative. Hugh Ross, for instance, cites Genesis 30:14: "days of the wheat harvest" and Joshua 24:7: "and you dwelt in the wilderness many days," to demonstrate that *yôm* can refer to an indefinite period of time.[71] In these cases, *yôm* certainly may mean an indefinite time. However, in most cases Ross cites, *yôm* occurs in construct with other nouns, which is a special syntactical relationship in the Hebrew. That syntax nowhere occurs with *yôm* in Genesis 1. Too, in those cases outside of Genesis 1 where such structural syntactical occurrences do occur with *yôm*, none of them can be construed to indicate millions or billions of years. More will be said about this later.

Because justification is not possible elsewhere in Scripture, some appeal to mere conjecture. Others appeal to the "Book of Creation," i.e., the claims of science, now to be elevated to a plain of authority equal to that of Scripture or even superior to Scripture if

---

[71] Hugh Ross, *Creation and Time*, 46.

necessary.[72] Yet it is the special revelation of Scripture that invests the general revelation of God in nature with any authority whatsoever (Ps. 19, Rom. 1). If the findings of science are to be elevated in authority over the Scripture, then the "Book of Creation" becomes God, and the Bible becomes null and void, except for those passages that elevate that Book of Creation. All other parts of Scripture that do not agree with changeable scientific conclusions will be relegated eventually to the category of mythology. This would include both the virgin birth and the resurrection of the Lord Jesus Christ, both of which events science concludes are impossible since they don't comport with modern empirical observations.

Seeing Genesis 1:1–2:3 as a special creation genre because of its uniqueness is at least possible, but there is nothing yet discovered among ancient inscriptions or manuscripts that can by comparison confirm that possibility. Unless and until such discoveries are made, I believe that prudence dictates that our interpretation of the passage should be constrained by intra–textual, intra–contextual, and intra–cultural studies within the ANE milieu. Science should be consulted, if at all, only after the proper biblical exegesis is completed. The results of science then should be subjected to the authority of Scripture, not the other way around.

Genesis 1:1–2:3 best fits within the known biblical genre of historical narrative, and should be taken normally and literally as communicating a very quick and recent creation, consistent with traditional understanding of six successive days of twenty-four-hours duration. The immediately following chapters are dedicated to the exegetical reasons foundational to this position.

---

[72] Cf. Patricia Williams, "Can Christianity Get Along without Adam and Eve?" *Research News & Opportunities in Science and Religion* 3:3 (November 2002): 20. Williams is only slightly ahead of the alarming trend in evangelicalism in denying the historicity of the creation, of Adam and Eve, and of the fall.

Five: "In the Beginning" Genesis 1:1–2

The very first word of the Hebrew Bible is controversial. The word *bᵉrēʾšîṯ* [lit., "in beginning"] is controversial because it is not written *bārēʾšîṯ* [lit., "in the beginning"].[73] The definite article "the" expected in this phrase would be indicated normally only by the Hebrew morpheme for an a–class vowel[74] In other words, since the definite article "the" is missing from the Hebrew word *bᵉrēʾšîṯ*, some prefer to translate it as "in a beginning," and as such consider the words to be open to interpretations other than a single, more recent beginning.[75]

The initial word *rēʾšîṯ* is formed from the root *rōʾš*, which has the basic meaning of "head."[76] It (*rēʾšîṯ*) has normally been translated as "beginning" or "chief." It is prefixed here with the preposition *bēṯ* which in this case means "in or "at" yielding the form we find in the text.

Since the word appears anarthrously (not having the definite article "the"), some have desired to see this phrase in construct with the finite verb *bārāʾ* (created), which immediately

---

73 One must note that the temporal noun *rēʾšîṯ* occurs only one time out of nearly fifty occurrences with an article. All other occurrences are without the definite article.

74 All first-year Hebrew students should recognize that this morpheme in the presence of an inseparable prefixed preposition is the sole remnant of the normally expected morpheme *ha* + doubling of the first letter (or, radical) of the root word. In this particular case, the *bēṯ* preposition overrides the *h* of the article, and the *paṯaḥ* (a) is lengthened as compensation in the presence of the initial letter *rēš* (this letter cannot normally be doubled) of the basic noun *rēʾšîṯ*. This process is more simply known as "compensatory lengthening" (see Thomas O. Lambdin, *Introduction to Biblical Hebrew*, Scribner's, 1971, xxi).

75 There are some early versions that reveal that the translators clearly did read the word as "in the beginning." For instance, this reading is affirmed by documents from the Cairo Geniza and by the Hexapla of Origen (cf. the textual apparatus of BHS at Genesis 1:1).

76 BDB, 910.

follows the initial *bᵉrē’šîṯ*. Allow me for the moment to explain what I mean by construct. Normally, a construct relationship exists in Hebrew between two nouns, not between a noun and a verb. It is a very close relationship and normally offers a genitival nuance. It is often called the "bound" relationship. Examples would include phrases such as "the son of the king," which in Hebrew would appear morphologically as "son the king," or, "the days of the barley harvest," which would appear in Hebrew only as "days the barley harvest."[77] In both of these examples above, one can see that in Hebrew the definite article "the" does not appear on the first word. This is normal Hebrew grammatical structure. However, definiteness in a construct chain is determined by the second noun.[78] Since "the" is present on the second noun in these examples, the entire phrase is definite.[79] Because the first word of Scripture *bᵉrē’šîṯ* does not have a definite article morphologically present, some would like to see it in construct with the second word *bārā’* (created),[80] which is actually a verb. Others would argue against this since it is a very unusual syntax to have a noun in construct with a finite verb. Unusual, yes, but it is not impossible. There are a small number of such cases in Scripture.[81] Assuming for the moment for the sake of argument that *bᵉrē’šîṯ* does stand in

---

77 For the first-year Hebrew student, there are also morphological/phonological and accentual changes that indicate the construct state in many of the initial nouns of a construct chain (Allen P. Ross, *Introducing Biblical Hebrew*, (Baker, 1999) 99, Bruce K. Waltke and M. O'Connor, *An Introduction to Biblical Hebrew Syntax*, (Eisenbraun's, 1990): 138).

78 For the first-year Hebrew student, definiteness on a noun may be determined in ways other than having an article: as the first noun of a construct chain, as a proper noun, and when suffixed with pronouns.

79 Lambdin, 68.

80 Young points out that *bᵉrē’šîṯ* normally occurs in the construct and thus appears without the article "the" (Edward J. Young, *Studies in Genesis 1*, 4). However, only in this verse and in Isaiah 46:10 does the noun *rē’šîṯ* stand alone apart from another noun, and outside of the possibility of this verse, it never appears in construct with a verb.

81 Young, 3, n. 7, cites as examples: Lev. 14:46; 1 Sam. 5:9, 25:15; Ps. 16:3; 58:9; 81:6; Isaiah 29:1; Hos. 1:2. One must note that 1 Samuel 5:9 is a fixed form preposition *’ăharê* followed by a verb, not a noun in construct with a verb. The example in Psalm 16:3 is a normal construct chain with no verb visible; that in 58:9 is textually uncertain. In none of the remaining examples cited is the verb an infinitive construct.

construct with the verb, some have wished instead to revocalize the finite verb *bārā'* as the infinitive construct form *b^{e}rō'*,[82] which is more grammatically acceptable, especially when temporal nouns are in view.[83] (Stay with me now, as I am attempting to put the argument in terms understandable for the interested layperson.) One must not confuse the "infinitive construct" with the "construct" relationship normally between nouns. The first is a verbal form with a particular verbal pattern that distinguishes it from finite verbs, participles, and infinitives absolute. Unlike a finite verb, infinitives construct can accept a prefixed preposition. Unlike the infinitive absolute, infinitives construct can take pronominal suffixes. If one could read the second word *bārā'* as the infinitive construct *b^{e}rō'* then a legitimate translation of the first three words including *'ĕlōhîm* (God) might be something like "in the beginning of God's creating," or simply "when God began to create." In both of these cases, the first verse would serve as a temporal clause dependent on verse 2, or possibly even verse 3 also to complete the thought. Either way, so translating allows for the *possibility* of other creations, earlier than that described in chapter 1. Thus there is an impetus that comes primarily from the ardent supporters of the old earth community to translate the first two or three words in this manner.

However, is it really necessary to do this? Better, would there be any reason to do this apart from modern interpretations of general revelation (the so–called "Book of Creation") as to the age of the earth? Let's examine another viewpoint.

---

[82] In this case, it was not Darwinism that led to this proposal; Rabbi Rashi proposed it in the AD twelfth century (Umberto Cassuto, *Genesis*, 19).

[83] For the first-year Hebrew student, Waltke's explanation that the presence of the *bēṯ* preposition in proximity with the infinitive construct indicates a temporal relationship pertains only to that preposition directly affixed to the infinitive construct, not prefixed to the initial noun of a construct chain (Waltke and O'Connor, 604).

First of all, *rē'šîṯ* (beginning) is a temporal noun. Adverbial temporal expressions (those indicating a timeframe) regularly occur without a definite article in biblical Hebrew, yet are translated as if they were definite (or even absolute) nouns. For instance, the same word *rē'šîṯ* occurs in Isaiah 46:10: "Making known from the beginning the end. . . ."[84] Though anarthrous (i.e., the definite article is not present in the text), the word *beginning* here is read as a definite noun (as if it had the article) in the NASV, NIV, RSV, and the KJV. The temporal noun *rô'š* , though anarthrous, is translated as "from the beginning" in Proverbs 8:23 (which Walther Eichrodt claims indicates an absolute use in parallel with "from eternity");[85] as are Ecclesiastes 3:11;[86] Isaiah 40:21 (in this case *mērô'š* "from of old," or "from the beginning" is synonymously parallel with the very definite "from the foundation of the earth"); [87] and Isaiah 41:4, 26. These are all examples of how a temporal noun is used in the absolute (thus, definite) sense without the morphological presence of the definite article. NASV and NIV at Isaiah 48:16 translate the same anarthrous form *mērô'š* as "from the first." In fact, most nouns that operate temporally do so in an anarthrous form in the Hebrew Bible, so it should not be unusual to find *bᵉrē'šîṯ* in that same manner in Genesis 1:1.[88]

Secondly, and stay with me here, when two nouns are in a construct relationship, the first in that construct chain, said to be the noun in construct, is always anarthrous, yet made

---

84 Unless otherwise noted, all translations from the Hebrew Bible are the author's.

85 Cited in Westermann, 98.

86 NIV differs from the other three versions at this point with "from beginning to end."

87 For the first-year Hebrew student, *mērô'š* is the word *rô'š* prefixed by the preposition *min,* the final *nun* of which has not been able to assimilate into the *rêš* as doubling, so it lengthens as compensation within its vowel class from the *ḥireq* to the *ṣērē.*

88 The noun *qedem,* when used temporally, is found without the article in Nehemiah 12:46; Isaiah 45:21; and 46:10 with the translation of "from of old," or "from antiquity." Thus also the term *ʿôlām* ("everlasting" "forever" Genesis 3:22 and numerous others) is anarthrous and may or may not be definite. Since these are general translations, it helps only to illustrate how temporal nouns are normally anarthrous.

definite (as if the article "the" was present) by the fact that it exists bound to the second noun (in the absolute form), specifying exactly which is being pointed out. Remember our examples? Phrases exist such as "the son of the king," which in Hebrew appears morphologically as "son the king;" or, "the days of the barley harvest," which appears in Hebrew only as "days the barley harvest." In both cases the first word is made definite by means of the close construct relationship with the second, even though the first word occurs anarthrously (without the definite article "the"), and is nonetheless consistently translated as if it had the article "the." This being the case, if *bᵉrēʾšîṯ* is indeed in construct with the second word *bārāʾ*, which happens to be a finite verb, the issue of definiteness/indefiniteness would be difficult to determine, since such appellations do not pertain to finite verbs.

Finally, Young points out that *bᵉrēʾšîṯ* is accented with the Hebrew disjunctive accent known as a *ṯip̄ḥâ*, which indicates that the word stands as an independent phrase, not in construct but rather as an absolute.[89] Thus, the Massoretes, who were zealous to preserve both the morphology and phonology of the text, would have been comfortable with our commonly held translation of "in the beginning."[90] Young also points out that no ancient versions of the Bible considered this word to be in construct with the verb that follows.[91]

Allow me to try to make sense of all of this concerning the first word of the Bible. Some have attempted to render the term *bᵉrēʾšîṯ* as being in the construct state with the verb

---

[89] Young, 5.

[90] For the second-year Hebrew students among you, Umberto Cassuto points out as well that if one were to construe verse 1 as a temporal clause dependent on verse 2, then the initial verb of verse 2, *hayᵉṯâ*, being presently in the second position of the sentence, would have been moved to the first position. Since this is not the case, then verse 1 must be independent of verse 2, which starts a new subject (Cassuto, *Genesis*, 19–20).

[91] Young, 5.

"to create," *bārāʾ*, which some arbitrarily wish to revocalize as *b^{e}rōʾ*.[92] All of this is done in order to render verse 1:1 as a temporal clause (the protosis) dependent on verse 1:2 as the apodosis and thus be able to translate the entire first verse as "when God began to create the heavens and the earth." *Thus, this rendering is in sharp disagreement with virtually all extant Hebrew manuscripts; in disagreement with every ancient translated version of the verse; in disagreement with the Massoretes entrusted to protect the letters and sounds of biblical Hebrew; in disagreement with the fact that nouns in construct with other nouns (and seemingly with finite verbs as well) are notoriously anarthrous, yet definite by that construct relationship itself; in disagreement with the Massoretic accentuation; and in disagreement with the verbal and clausal structure of verse 2. From a grammatical, historical, syntactical, and structural analysis of the phrase that begins with b^{e}rēʾšîṯ, I can see no possible reason derived from special revelation, i.e., from the inscripturated Word of God, for anyone to translate the phrase as "in a beginning" or "when God began to create."* Those who would do so today could be attempting to elevate the "Book of Creation" (read: current interpretations of empirical data) above the Book of God's Word, the Bible.

Having therefore established the proper understanding of *b^{e}rēʾšîṯ* as "In the beginning," we need to move on to the rest of verse 1. The second word of the Bible is *bārāʾ*. This verb, which basically means "to create," is a God word. By that I mean that the verb is found in all of its thirty-five+ Old Testament appearances in the basic Qal stem (from *qālal*, to be light, or unencumbered) with God as the subject of the action displayed by the verb.

---

[92] This conjecture is made without any extant alternative reading in any known manuscript as textual support to do so.

Even when appearing in the passive Niphal stem, God is still the sole agent of the activity (Exod. 34:10; Ps. 148:5; Ezek. 28:13).[93] The verb *bārā'* is at times used synonymously with the common verb *'āśâ* ("to make, to do"), which has been noted as something that man is also able to do. The fact is nonetheless true that only God can *bārā'* (create). In my opinion, the presence (in and of itself) of the verb in the Qal stem neither confirms nor denies *Creatio Ex Nihilo* (Latin for: "creation out of nothing").[94] However, Young points out that the verb may be seen with the accusative of product (in other words, that which God is creating), but never with the material used being mentioned.[95]

Since *bārā'* is a God word, one expects to find the subject in this case to be God, as it is. The third word of the Bible is just that: *'ĕlōhîm*, and though *b^erē'šîṯ* has the preeminent position in the verse for emphasis, *'ĕlōhîm* is the central character of the narrative, inasmuch as He is the subject of the verb "create" and is presented as the ultimate first cause, existing before His creation and separate from it. I have written elsewhere:

> In perhaps what was meant as a polemic against the myths of the other nations, Genesis names *'elōhîm* . . . as the sole creator of all there is, not from a process of violence, but simply by the power of the spoken word (cf. 1:3, 6, 9, 11, 14, 20, 26). Another option would be to see the Genesis account as primary, with ANE mythologies deriving from it.

---

[93] For the first-year Hebrew students: only in the Piel stem (normally the intensifying verbal stem) does the basic gloss of "to create" and the subjects of the verb deviate from this observation, inasmuch as it is rendered in those few cases as "to cut down" or "to cut out." In my thinking, this gloss for the Piel stem is enough that perhaps a homonym *bērē'* should be separated from *bārā'* in the lexicons, unless of course one views the creation as light cut out of the darkness, heavens cut out of the waters, dry land cut out of the seas, flora cut out of the soil, fish cut out of the waters, birds cut out of the heavens, land animals cut out of the ground, and man cut out of the clay.

[94] David M. Fouts, "Genesis 1–11," in the *Bible Knowledge Key Word Study*, ed. by Eugene H. Merrill, Cook, 2003, 40. Allen Ross agrees, *Creation and Blessing*, 106.

[95] It therefore becomes the verb of choice in Young's thinking for describing the absolute creation. By this, I believe him to mean that the presence of the verb in 1:1 indicates *creatio ex nihilo* (Young, 6–7). My own opinion is that *creatio ex nihilo* may be involved with the use of *bārā'* in 1:1, inasmuch as the author to the Hebrews must have understood this to be the case as he penned Hebrews 11:3: "By faith we understand that the worlds were prepared by the word of God, so that what is seen was not made out of things which are visible" (NASV).

> The divine *'elōhîm* is seen in the OT as righteous (Ps. 7:9), as holy (Josh. 24:19), as living (Jer. 10:10), as everlasting (Isa. 40:28), as true (2 Chron. 15:3). He is the God of Abraham, Isaac, and Jacob (Genesis 26:24; Exod. 3:6; Ps. 47:9), and called the God of Israel (Genesis 33:20) and the God of the Hebrews (Exod. 5:3). He is the God of all flesh (Jer. 32:27). For the believer, He is a rock of protection (2 Sam. 22:3; cf. Ps. 43:2), He is the source of righteousness (Ps. 4:1), He is the God of salvation (Ps. 18:46; Isaiah 17:10; Mic. 7:7; Hab. 3:18), and He is our praise (Ps. 109:1).[96]

This is the God who created in the beginning. That which He created at the beginning is the topic of the next few paragraphs.

That which God created in the beginning is named as "the heavens and the earth," *ʾēt haššāmayim wᵉʾēṯ hāʾāreṣ.*[97] The two nouns form a figure of speech called a *merism*, which is indicated by naming two extremes in order to indicate totality.[98] As an example, in Ps. 1:2 the happy man meditates on the Torah "by day and by night," meaning "continually." Basically, when it is said that God created the heavens and the earth, it means that God created the heavens, the earth, and everything in between (cf. Exod. 20:11). This specific application of *merism* is common among all languages, according to Westermann.[99] Young says that the terms juxtaposed in this manner are used to convey the universe in its entirety,[100] as does Allen Ross.[101] As such, all efforts to equate this occurrence of either the earth or the heavens with the same terms elsewhere in the passage before us will fail. Both the term earth, *'ereṣ,* and the term heavens, *šāmayim,* will each separately have differing

---

[96] Fouts, op.cit., 39.

[97] For the first-year Hebrew students: the vocalization of *'ereṣ* to *'āreṣ* is due to vowel harmonization in the presence of the definite article.

[98] Allen P. Ross, *Creation and Blessing*, Baker, 1988, 106.

[99] Claus Westermann, *Genesis 1–11: A Continental Commentary*, trans. John J. Scullion, (Fortress, 1994): 101.

[100] Young, 9.

[101] Allen P. Ross, 106.

nuances within the text of Genesis 1:1–2:3, and thus will be analyzed on a case by case basis in the discussion below.[102]

Genesis 1:1 therefore reveals that God existed from before the creation began (cf. John 1:1). This same God lauded throughout Scripture created everything that exists in six sequential days at the very beginning of the universe as we know it, as we shall see below. Young writes: "Hence, we may understand the writer as asserting that the heaven and earth had a beginning and that this beginning is to be found in the fact that God had created them."[103]

What then is the relationship between verse 1 with the rest of the creation pericope (1:1–2:3)? We have seen already that it is unlikely that the first word, *bᵉrēʾšîṯ*, should be understood in construct with the finite verb *bārāʾ*; that it should be understood instead as an absolute temporal noun expressing simply "in the beginning." Therefore the first verse cannot serve as subordinate to a main verb in 1:2. In other words, the first verse stands alone, apart from the rest of the text. There are two other choices. The first choice is that 1:1 states that God created everything, which resulted initially in the condition expressed in 1:2, which by the way does not have the designation of "good." The second choice is that 1:1 serves as a topic sentence to the section, and 1:2 simply states the state of things that existed when God began His creative work on day 1. That 1:1 should be thus understood is supported by typical Hebrew narrative in general and in the structural indicators in Genesis specifically.[104] Though there are difficulties with either structural analysis, I take the verse as a topic

---

[102] We will find the same thing is true for *yôm*, which is used in five differing ways in the same section.

[103] Young, 7.

[104] Genesis is marked structurally by the *tôlᵉdôṯ* formula seen in the English translation: "These are the generations of" which phrase occurs in 2:4; 5:1; 6:9; 10:1; 11:27; 25:12; 25:19; 36:1; and 37:2 at the beginning of significant pericopes of material. The phrase is conspicuously absent in 1:1–2:3, a fact that has caused some to understand 1:1 as conveying a similar function.

sentence for the section 1:2–2:3, a reasonable position held by numerous Old Testament scholars.[105]

The Earth before God Spoke

Verse 1:2 begins recounting specifically the details of the story introduced by the statement of 1:1. Syntactically distinct from 1:1, verse 2 reveals the condition of the earth when God began speaking in 1:3. The verse is introduced by a *wāw* (normally meaning "and"), which many translations take to be a *wāw* disjunctive ("now") in this case inasmuch as it is prefixed to the noun *hā'āreṣ* (the earth) rather than to the verb *hāy^e^ṯâ* (was). This type of construction normally indicates the introducing of a new section or a parenthetical phrase. Other examples of the *wāw* disjunctive in Genesis include 12:6b: "Now the Canaanite was then in the land"; 13:2: "Now Abram was very wealthy with moveable property, with silver, and with gold"; and 13:13: "Now the men of Sodom were very wicked and sinners against the Lord." About the use of the *wāw* disjunctive in 1:2, Cassuto has written:

> Whenever the subject comes before the predicate, as here, the intention of the Bible is to give emphasis to the subject and to tell us something new about it. Here, too, the meaning is: "As for the earth alluded to in the first verse, I must tell you that at the beginning of its creation, it was without form or life. . ."[106]

Nothing is revealed about how this inhospitable condition came to be, but the terms in the passage are often used elsewhere in Scripture to suggest judgment, troubled times, or difficulties. Again, there is no designation of the condition being good until God commands "light" to be. Nothing is said specifically about the heavens, which are yet to be formed in

---

[105] A. Ross, 105; Waltke, *Creation and Chaos*, 1974, 36; Cassuto, *Genesis*, 20. Westermann, *Genesis,* 97: "The first verse then is to be understood as a principal sentence. The creation of the world by God is expressed in one sentence as in the praise of God. And because this sentence is prefixed to the actual account of creation it acquires monumental importance which distinguishes it from other creation stories." Rooker has recently developed the other viewpoint (Mark F. Rooker, "Genesis 1:1–3: Creation or Re–Creation? Part 1," *Bibliotheca Sacra* 149 (1992) 316–23; "Part 2," *Bibliotheca Sacra* 149 (1992): 411–27).

[106] Cassuto, *Genesis*, 21.

response to God's command.[107] But something existed, and it is called *'ereṣ*, but certainly cannot be *'ereṣ* in the same sense that it would be six days later, so it seems that the term is broad enough to include both an uninhabitable place as well as a totally ordered and habitable world. The words of St. Peter that "by the word of God the heavens existed long ago and the earth was formed out of water and by water" (2 Pet. 3:5 NASV) are confirmed by the terms "the deep", *t^ehôm,* and "waters", *mayim,* in 1:2. So one may say that the earth as described in 1:2 was covered with water. One may also infer from 1:9 that these waters covered land surfaces that were to appear on the third day.

The Gap theory, popularized by the Scofield Reference edition Bible of 1909, was developed in part to explain how the condition in 1:2 came to be. It suggested there that there was a world prior to the creation of 1:2–2:3 that was ruled by Satan because of whom the entire world was destroyed in the wake of that demon's rebellion. The view is supported grammatically by understanding that the verb *hāy^eṯâ* should be translated actively as "had become" rather than as a stative "was." The view also explains the nouns of the verse that seem to indicate judgment and troubled times.[108] It claims to explain as well the fossil record of the geologic column that was becoming a greater part of daily conversation at the end of the nineteenth and beginning of the twentieth centuries, therefore allowing for a harmonization of Scripture and science. However, the Gap theory has been thoroughly refuted for many reasons, many of which will be discussed below in the analysis of key terms.[109]

---

[107] Cassuto (ibid.) says that the "heavens" are mentioned first in verse 1 because of their greater importance, but that the focus of 1:2–2:3 is upon the earth. Hence, the earth is described first in 1:2.

[108] The terms darkness and the deep elsewhere in Scripture often have nuances of troubled times.

[109] For an in–depth critique of the Gap theory, see Weston W. Fields, *Unformed and Unfilled*, Burgerner Enterprises, 1976.

The main verb of verse 2 is *hāyᵉṯâ*. This form, from the root *hāyâ*, normally is understood as the stative verb "to be." When translated actively, i.e., as "to become," the syntax often appears as the verb followed by the direct object prefixed by the *lamedh* preposition, as in 1 Samuel 22:2: "He became (form of *hāyâ* followed by *lamedh*) prince over them."[110] Admittedly, when the *lamedh* is absent, context can indicate the active nuance of "to become," but such cases are unusual.

Those who support the Gap theory argue that the verb *hāyᵉṯâ* should be translated with the active sense, and also should be understood as a past perfect (or, "pluperfect" in some grammars). In other words, it should be translated, "now the earth *had become* formless and void. . . ." One must concede that, grammatically, the verbal form itself can go either as a simple past of the stative verb: "now the earth was . . ." or as the past perfect "now the earth had become." However, for it to be a past perfect there must be the proper setting. In the proximate context there must be a main verb in the past tense, in order to indicate that the action of the past perfect chronologically precedes the action of the main verb, i.e., some statement or event to which the past perfect provides a setting.[111] Since this situation does not occur in verse 2, and cannot be the *bārāʾ* of the topic sentence in verse 1 (which as we have seen stands alone) nor the initial verb of 1:3 (which continues the narrative sequencing), the translation "now the earth had become" is likely not possible.[112]

Of continuing discussion among scholars and laypersons alike is the precise meaning of *tōhû wāḇōhû*. This term has been translated in many ways, from "formless and void"

[110] BDB, 226.

[111] Such a case occurs in Genesis 24:45 and 24:62–63.

[112] For the Hebrew student: the fact that verse 3 begins with a waw consecutive form confirms this, as a waw consecutive preterite cannot follow a pluperfect without functioning itself as a pluperfect.

(NASV), to "without form and void" (RSV); to "unformed and unfilled";[113] to "formless and empty" (NIV); to "formlessness and emptiness";[114] to many others.

Before analyzing the constituent parts, it must be said that some view this phrase as *hendiadys*, where two closely related nouns are joined by a simple *wāw* to express a single concept (in this case a "formless void").[115]

Now I do not wish to spend much time on the various suggested meanings of *tōhû wāḇōhû*, since that discussion may be found in the numerous commentaries on Genesis 1. Instead, I will offer a summarizing quote followed by a few observations. The *Bible Knowledge Word Study* offers:

> The first term occurs far more frequently than the second, which occurs a total of three *x*. The use of the two terms together in Jer. 4:23 is probably an allusion to the Genesis account applied by the prophet to the destruction of Jerusalem and Judah at the time of Nebuchadnezzar's third invasion in 586 BC. Isaiah 34:11 employs both terms and predicts a similar wasting of Edom. Alone, tōhû can refer to a wasteland (Deut. 32:10; Job 6:18), empty arguments (Isaiah 29:21) and idols that have no substance (1 Sam. 12:21; Isaiah 41:29). Even idol–makers accomplish nothing (Isaiah 44:9). The emphasis in this passage then seems to be that the earth then existed with no purpose, it had no value, it was not yet ready to sustain the life that God was about to bring about.[116]

Many point to Isaiah 45:18, which affirms that God did not make the earth to be a "waste place" (*tōhû*) but rather to be inhabited. The focus of this statement by Isaiah is to demonstrate the purpose of creating the earth in the first place: it was for His creatures. This indicates that it was not created to *remain* a "waste place." Thus, our verse in 1:2 does not state whether God created it as formless waste to begin with, or if it somehow became that

[113] Fields, *Unformed and Unfilled,* 113.
[114] Allen P. Ross, *Creation and Blessing*, 106.
[115] Fields, 124.
[116] David M. Fouts, "Genesis 1–11," 40.

way in some manner such as judgment. Scripture is silent at this point, and it is perhaps best to leave it that way.

The narrator then tells us, perhaps as explaining the *tōhû wāḇōhû,* that "darkness covered the surface of the deep," *wᵉḥōšeḵ ʿal–pᵉnê tᵉhôm.* Two terms here need to be addressed. The first term to be considered is darkness, *ḥōšeḵ*. At times, *ḥōšeḵ* is simply the opposite of light, as it seems to be here with 1:3 in proximate context. Isaiah 45:7 affirms this in that God created both light and darkness. At other times, *ḥōšeḵ* is used as a metaphor for difficult situations of life, or turbulent times. In Job 19:8, Job replies to Bildad: "He has walled up my way so that I cannot pass; and He has put darkness on my paths" (NASV). Ecclesiastes 11:8 reminds mankind to rejoice in the years of life because there will be plenty of days of darkness to endure as well. In Isaiah 5:30, darkness and distress are closely associated. Of course, there is also the classic connection of darkness with judgment in God's ninth plague on the Egyptians (Ex. 10:21–22). Since the context of Genesis 1:2 does not indicate any judgment, and the remainder of Scripture is silent on it, and since the context offers a simple contrast of light in 1:3, it is perhaps best not to conjecture further.[117]

The narrator informs us that this darkness covered the surface of the deep (*tᵉhôm*). Formerly, many have seen in this word the name of the Akkadian goddess Tiamat, who according to the *Enuma Elish* ruled over the primeval oceans and was later defeated by Marduk who created the heavens and the earth from Tiamat's body.[118] Many now see that the

[117] Though Isaiah 14 probably only refers to demonic powers behind the king of Babylon, Ezekiel 28 probably does have Satan in view: "you were in Eden, the Garden of God." If this is the case, then his fall must have postdated the planting of the garden in Eden in Genesis 2:8, and thus cannot be the cause of the state of the earth described in Genesis 1:2.

[118] See Cassuto's explanation (Cassuto, 23).

two terms *t^ehôm* and *tiamat* both derived from an earlier proto–Semitic form.[119] Allen Ross has said that the "deep" is not spoken in Genesis 1 "in mythological terms: it is simply the primeval ocean and not a goddess in rebellion."[120] This conforms to an examination of the usages of the term throughout the remainder of the Old Testament, with both subterranean and oceanic "depths" being in view.[121]

As the narrator continues in 1:2, we are informed that "the Spirit of God was hovering over the surface of the waters," *wᵉrûaḥ ʾĕlōhîm mᵉraḥepeṯ ʿal–pᵉnê hammāyim.* Instead of the term "spirit of God," (*rûaḥ ʾĕlōhîm*), "a mighty wind" has been accepted by many as the preferred translation in keeping with, and supplementing, the description of the first two clauses of 1:2.[122] Cassuto does not understand it this way but thinks the phrase must refer to God in some sense. He sees that "mighty wind" is not an appropriate subject for the word *mᵉraḥepeṯ*, which functions as a participle from the root *rāḥap.*[123] This verb indicates a hovering, such as in the brooding of an eagle over her nest.[124] Deuteronomy 32:11 reveals that God is similarly moved to care for His people. Thus the phrase should be understood as "the spirit of God" rather than "a mighty wind." In this case, it indicates that God is prepared to act to make an uninhabitable earth habitable.

[119] Westermann, *Genesis*, 105.
[120] Allen Ross, *Creation and Blessing*, 107.
[121] David M. Fouts and Kurt Wise, "Blotting Out and Breaking Up: Miscellaneous Hebrew Studies in Geocatastrophism," in *Proceedings of the Fourth International Conference on Creationism: Technical Symposium Sessions*, ed. Robert E. Marsh, 1998, 222.
[122] Westermann, 107, claims that W. F. Albright, H. M. Orlinsky, Gerhard von Rad, W. H. Schmidt, and E. A. Speiser all take this view.
[123] Cassuto, 24.
[124] Allen Ross, 107.

Six: God Speaks and the Earth Is Changed Genesis 1:3–5

To summarize what has been said to this point, Genesis 1:1 offers a topic sentence introducing the narrative of God's creative activities. Verse 2 serves to provide the setting of darkness over water that covers an uninhabitable earth. All is under the care of the Spirit of God, so when God speaks in verse 3, this situation begins to improve.

It becomes necessary to deal with the initial phrase of Genesis 1:3: "and God said" (*wayyō'mer 'elōhîm*). The same phrase occurs ten times in the chapter, and anchors the repeated cycle of command, fulfillment, assessment, and time indication. The verb *'āmar* ("say, speak"), the root of the form *wayyō'mer,* is extremely common in the MT, but since it is God speaking here, the concept of the spoken word of God is introduced for the first time in Scripture.[125] One need only think of two passages to be reminded of the importance and authority of God's Word. Isaiah 55:11 informs us that God's word does not go out without accomplishing that for which He sent it. This is the efficacy of the divine "word." The initial verses of the gospel of John are also vital: "In the beginning was the Word, and the Word was with God, and the Word was God. He was in the beginning with God. All things came into being through Him, and apart from Him nothing came into being that has come into

[125] The noun *dābār* (word) is not found until Genesis 11:1.

being" (John 1:1–3) and "the Word became flesh, and dwelt among us" (John 1:14). These verses describe the divine power in the person of Christ, the Word incarnate.

In the Old Testament, the word of God came to Moses after it had first come to Abraham, Isaac, and Jacob. The word of God came to David through Nathan the prophet. The word of God came to Jonah, to Ezekiel, and to all the prophets. The evidence for the importance of the Word of God spoken, written, and incarnated is overwhelming in the passages of the Bible. And this importance is founded in chapter 1 of Genesis, as God speaks and light dispels the darkness in obedience to His command.

The fact that God commanded and that there was a response is worthy of comment. Clarence Darrow, a world renown defense attorney and noted atheist who led the defense of John Thomas Scopes in Dayton, Tennessee, in 1925, once remarked at the trial that: "Genesis, or the Bible, says nothing whatever about the method of creation."[126] Apparently Darrow regarded the decrees of God in creation to be figures of speech, as he did with the narrative of the creation of Adam in Genesis 2:7: "We say that God created man out of the dust of the earth is simply a figure of speech."[127] However, the decrees themselves are important to investigate, if one is to take the text normally with a grammatical–historical interpretation, because they do establish the process of creation: it was by divine command. Peter the apostle believed this as well: "...by the word of God *the* heavens existed long ago and *the* earth was formed out of water and by water" (2 Pet. 3:5).

That the words of God on the creation days are decrees (or, commands) may be easily seen in the grammatical forms used. These forms are called jussives by most Hebrew grammarians.

---

126 *The World's Most Famous Court Trial*, Original transcript of the Scopes Trial, 2nd reprint edition (Dayton, TN: Bryan College, 199): 188.
127 Ibid.

The Jussives of Genesis 1

The verbal forms of the decrees of God in Genesis 1 traditionally have been understood as jussives.[128] In fact, most of these occurrences in chapter 1 must be understood that way because of morphology (their written form). Jussives of weak verbs,[129] as are found frequently in this passage, are often grammatically indicated in Hebrew by a shortened form of the imperfect tense. They are thus readily identifiable, either by the shortened form (such is the case for "let there be" *yᵉhî* in 1:3, 1:6, and 1:14, all from "to be" *hāyâ*), or from differing vowel patterning (as for instance the Hebrew words for "sprout" in 1:11 and "bring forth" in 1:12, 1:24). The verbs "let . . . be gathered" (1:9), "let . . . teem" and "let. . .fly" (1:20) in the decretive formulas are likewise thought to be jussives although the form of those words in the text before us is inconclusive morphologically. In other words, in other settings it could be difficult to determine from their morphology whether they were to be understood as imperfects or jussives. However, consistent within the stylized structure and repetition in the passage, as well as the numerous other jussives used on days 1–4, understanding them as jussives here is the preferred choice. Too, at least in the case of one of these in 1:9 ("let the waters be gathered"), the statement of completion ("and it was so") is given, suggesting a jussive nuance to that verb (as opposed to a specific future imperfect which might otherwise be understood to predict the future).

[128] Jussives are seen in 1:3, 1:6, 1:9, 1:11, 1:12, 1:14, 1:20, 1:24, 1:26. It is interesting to note at this point that creation decrees issued by any god are unique to Genesis 1 among ANE cosmogonies (David T. Tsumura, "Genesis and Ancient Near Eastern Stories of Creation and Flood: An Introduction," in *I Studied Inscriptions from Before the Flood*, eds. Richard S. Hess and David Toshio Tsumura, {Eisenbraun's, 1994}, 31).
[129] Note to Hebrew students, the weak verbs are final *hē* verbs, geminate verbs, and hollow verbs.

Chart: The Jussives of Command in Genesis 1

> And God said,
> Let there be light, and there was light
> Let there be an expanse . . . so God made the expanse
> Let the waters be gathered . . . and it was so.
> Let the earth sprout vegetation . . . and it was so
> Let there be lights . . . so God made the lights (2x)
> Let the waters teem . . . and God created them
> Let the earth bring forth animals . . . and it was so.

Having now established that the verbal forms used to express the manner of God's speaking on the days of creation are jussives, primarily identified by morphology and context, our discussions now must examine the syntactical nuances of jussives.

Jussives may be one of two types in biblical Hebrew. Though there are no morphological differences between these two types, the two are distinguished by context. These are called the jussive of command and the jussive of request.[130] A jussive of request is offered from an inferior to a superior, a jussive of command is offered from a superior to an inferior.

It is most likely that the jussives in Genesis 1 must be understood as jussives of command rather than jussives of request, since the Bible is consistent in depicting no one greater in power and authority than the Lord, the God of creation. So when God Himself as Creator commanded, His domain had no choice but to obey. This may be illustrated by Jesus who commanded the stormy waters of the Sea of Galilee: "He rebuked the wind and said to the sea, 'Hush, be still.' And the wind died down and it became perfectly calm" (Mark 4:39). To this miracle, the disciples responded, "Who then is this, that even the wind and the sea obey Him?" (Mark 4:41).

---

[130] Allen P. Ross, *Introducing Biblical Hebrew*, 150.

It would probably be instructive at this point to digress to a related issue, that of commands in the Bible. It seems in Scripture that the more power held by a king, the faster his commands were carried out. Such was the case with Pharaoh in Genesis 41:14: "Then Pharaoh sent and called for Joseph, and they hurriedly brought him out of the dungeon …." and for Ahasuerus in Esther 7:8: "As soon as the word went from the king's mouth, they covered Haman's face." In Daniel 2:12–13, Nebuchadnezzar's power was seen in the response of his servants to his commands: ". . . (the king) gave orders to destroy all the wise men of Babylon. So the decree went forth that the wise men should be slain; and they looked for Daniel and his friends to kill them."

Even in the New Testament, the power held by Herod Antipas is witnessed by the quickness with which his commands were carried out: "And immediately the king sent an executioner and commanded him to bring his head. And he went and had him beheaded in the prison" (Mark 6:27).[131] The same seems to be true with Jesus, the King of Kings, in His earthly ministry:

> Then He arose, and rebuked the winds and the sea; and it became perfectly calm (Matt. 8, Mark 4, Luke 8).
>
> And He stretched out His hand, and touched him, saying, "I am willing; be cleansed." And immediately the leprosy left him (Luke 4).
>
> But Jesus rebuked the unclean spirit, and healed the boy, and gave him back to his father. And they were all amazed at the greatness of God (Luke 9).

More work remains in this area, particularly in observing possible patterning in the jussives of command that may be present in other parts of the Bible and in analogous expressions in other ANE inscriptions. It is certainly interesting to note that Jesus, God

---

[131] All NT citations are from the NASV.

incarnate, the one who exegetes God, the King of Kings, operates almost always instantaneously in His miraculous dealings.[132] Should we therefore expect God the Father to work any slower? Indeed, the psalmist affirms the swiftness of the issued Word of God when he says: "He who sends forth His command (*'imrâ* [root *'āma*r]), as quickly His word (*dābār*) runs" (Ps. 147:15).

God issued the command "Let there be light" as the starting point of the creation process. There was immediate response within His domain: "and light was." But how can this be, when according to the text, there is not yet a sun? Scientists may say that this is physically impossible, as physical light cannot exist apart from a physical source. Yet with God, all things are possible, Jesus said (Luke 18:27). Now before someone objects to my use of this verse, I am well aware that the context of Luke 18 has to do with the salvation of man by God and thus may not be able to be used in support of the physical possibility of light apart from the sun. However, I would again appeal to these words of Christ when He healed the paralytic lowered through the roof. In this case, He affirmed by word and by example that the forgiveness of man's sinfulness (i.e., salvation) was a far more difficult task than mere physical healing. With the God presented in the Bible, all things *are* possible, even when modern empirical observations are not in agreement. When Sarah laughed derisively at the announcement of her impending pregnancy with Isaac, God retorted: "Is there anything too wonderful for God?" (Gen. 18:14).

Concerning light existing apart from the physical presence of the sun, there are some scriptural examples to consider. For instance, Psalm 104:2 reveals that God cloaks Himself with light. Isaiah 60:19 informs Israel that they will ultimately have no need of the sun: "No

---

[132] In fact, the only impediment to universal obedience to God's commands or those of His Son Jesus seems to be sourced in the sinfulness of humanity.

longer will you have the sun for light by day, nor for brightness will the moon give you light; but you will have the Lord for an everlasting light, and your God for your glory." First John 1:5 states that God is light. Revelation 21:23 indicates that in heaven, no sun is necessary, for it is the glory of God Himself that illumines the new earth where there is no darkness. This latter passage by the way forms an *inclusio* with the light without a sun offered in Genesis 1:3, tying the first and last books of Scripture together nicely.

Though not absolutely conclusive in the discussion, there may be support for the possibility of light existing without the physical presence of the sun in the pages of Egyptian mythology. Gordon Johnston, associate professor of Old Testament studies at Dallas Seminary, recently wrote an article on "Genesis 1 and Ancient Egyptian creation Myths" for the DTS journal *Bibliotheca Sacra*. Taking his lead from A. H. Sayce,[133] Johnston writes:

> According to the tradition of Hermopolis the first creative act was the emergence of light from the primeval gloom and darkness. After millions of years of the darkness of the primeval waters, the god Atum (later Rê–Atum) evolved/emerged out of Nun. As the sun–god his first act was to manifest himself as light—before he formally created the sun.[134]

This passage may reflect exposure to the early Hebrew traditions now recorded in Genesis 1 and incorporated into the Egyptian mythology. On the other hand, if the Genesis account postdates the Egyptian texts (the viewpoint of most scholars)[135] then the biblical version could stand as a polemic against the earlier Egyptian myth while affirming this one point of

---

[133] A. H. Sayce, "The Egyptian Background of Genesis 1," in *Studies Presented to F. Ll. Griffith* (London: Egypt Exploration Society, 1932): 419–23.

[134] Gordon H. Johnston, "Genesis 1 and Ancient Egyptian Creation Myths," *Bibliotheca Sacra* 165 (2008): 186.

[135] P. J. Wiseman, *New Discoveries in Babylonia about Genesis*, 1936, believed that Genesis was handed down in tablet form from very ancient times.

agreement (i.e., that the creation of light preceded the creation of the luminaries) as being true.[136]

We reiterate that in the new heavens and new earth as recorded in the book of Revelation that there is no need for the sun, as God himself will provide the light (Rev. 21:23). So, with the God of the Bible, the problem of light existing apart from the sun is not a problem at all.

Genesis 1:3–5 begins the first of the cycles of command, fulfillment, assessment and time passage that recurs throughout the passage in essentially the same manner. The three excurses below will examine in greater depth the meaning of "day," "evening and morning," and "it was so."

Excursus: The Importance of *yôm* in Genesis 1:1–2:3

A traditional understanding in both Judaism and Christianity has been that Genesis 1:1–2:3 records the very recent and quick creation of the heavens and earth by the God of the Old Testament. In great part, this is due to reading the texts with a normal hermeneutic, trusting that the scholars who provided us with translations in our native tongues were not only intelligent and well educated but also honorable individuals. With the growing numbers of evangelicals who hold to Progressive Creationism or Theistic Evolution, either of which could be considered an "old earth" view, it is important for us to restudy the words of Scripture to establish a solid foundation for our discussion. Waltke has written: "In order to meet the challenge of science against the first chapter of Genesis, the apologist must have a

[136] Johnston (183–84) records up to eleven points of structural agreement, depending on which Egyptian tradition is in view.

clear understanding of the biblical cosmogony."[137] Hugh Ross, a popular and highly regarded proponent of the old earth creationist school, has stated:

> The first chapter of Genesis declares that within six "days" God miraculously transformed a "formless and void" earth into a suitable habitat for mankind. The meaning of the word *day*, here, has become the center of a controversy. Does it, or does it not, make for a conflict between scripture and science?
>
> The answer to that question depends upon whether the time periods indicated are twenty-four-hours or, rather, something on the order of millions of years. Most Bible scholars (and scientists, too) would agree that a correct and literal interpretation of the creation "day" is one that takes into account definitions, context, grammar, and relevant passages from other parts of scripture. A careful analysis of all these elements yields many reasons for interpreting the creation days of Genesis as long periods of time.[138]

Since many on both sides of the issue would agree that the proper understanding of both the meaning and syntax of day (*yôm*) is absolutely crucial to the discussion, it is necessary for us now to begin the investigation just at that point.

The Five Ways *yôm* Is Used in Genesis 1:1–2:3[139]

Daytime (or Daylight)

The word day, *yôm*, is used as in apposition to and as an equivalent of daytime in Genesis 1:5. One notes here that it is God Himself who is naming the period of light as *yôm*, in contrast to the period of darkness that He names night, *lāylâ*.[140] That "daytime" should be understood for *yôm* is repeated in 1:14 where "day" is contrasting with "night." Similarly, in 1:16 where the greater light was "to rule" over the day, *yôm* means "daytime," as it does also

---

[137] Bruce K. Waltke, "The Creation Account in Genesis 1:1–3, Part II: The Restitution Theory," *BibSac* 132 (1975): 136. To this he added (137): "how we understand the syntax of Genesis 1:1–3 has a significant effect on our theology."

[138] Hugh Ross, *The Fingerprint of God*, second edition, (Reasons to Believe, 1991): 146.

[139] I will include 2:4 in this discussion because of its use of *yôm* in proximity to the uses of the same in 1:1–2:3.

[140] This fact should be important in the discussion. It is God who does the naming of the sequence of light and darkness as day and night respectively, showing His dominion over them.

in 1:18. "Daytime" may therefore legitimately gloss *yôm*, and when it does, it would not refer to a twenty-four-hour period, but rather that period where light shines, normally averaging a 12 hour period. Some have suggested that since this is the first use of the term in the Bible, it sets the standard upon which all other usages are based.

As a Clear Measurement of Time Passage

The term *yôm* is found in Genesis 1:14 with the meaning of calendar "days" in the phrase which expresses one of the purposes of the heavenly bodies: to be "for signs and for seasons and for days and years." In this case, there is no question of the use of *yôm* as a normal twenty-four-hour day.[141] This is true even if one interprets the appearance of *yôm* in this verse as referring specifically to special religious days involving fasting or feasting.

With Cardinal Numbers

One occurrence of *yôm* in our passage is with a cardinal number, specifically, "one" (*ʾeḥāḏ*) in 1:5. An ordinal (expressing order) is probably not used here because there were no other days (yet) with which to compare it.[142] A study of any exhaustive concordance reveals that all other occurrences of the phrase *yôm ʾeḥāḏ* indicate activities within a twenty-four-

---

[141] It is at least possible in my thinking that with the potential effects of the cataclysm of the deluge of Noah that a rotation of the earth revealing the presence of the sun and moon may or may not have been of twenty-four-hours duration in the pre–flood days. However, with the other terms used in the passage (as will be discussed below) and with the understanding of the author of the passage and that of later tradents as well, one doubts the possibility that the length of time passage that comprised a day of Genesis 1:1–2:3 would have been significantly different than that which we now experience. In other words, if it were widely known and believed that the passage of time involved in these "days" was significantly different than those of the readers, other words depicting lengthier periods were available to the Hebrews who repeated the account to succeeding generations.

[142] Cassuto, *Genesis,* 30.

hour period of time.[143] Too, the examples of the plural form *yāmîm* that occur with cardinal numbers elsewhere in narrative all refer to twenty-four-hour days (or portions thereof).

With Ordinal Numbers

The use of the term *yôm* with the ordinal numbers (1:8, 13, 19, 23; 2:2, 3) presents one of the major difficulties in the debate of the length of time involved for the activities of the creation account. For many, the sixth day presents an inordinate amount of activities to have occurred within a twenty-four-hour time span. For instance, Waltke is perturbed by the order and number of events that occurred on day six of the creation week, particularly in regard to the necessary speedy growth of the trees.[144] Gleason Archer writes similarly.[145] Among other things they are concerned with the amount of time that it may have taken for Adam to have named all the animals before Eve was created. These concerns will be addressed later in this book.

The term *yôm* occurs quite frequently with ordinal numbers elsewhere in the OT (Ex. 19:11, Lev. 13:5; Est. 9:1; and many other examples). In every case that *yôm* occurs in the singular with ordinal numbers in the hebrew Old Testament, it indicates a twenty-four-hour day—with possibly one exception. Norm Geisler, another well respected evangelical author and speaker, has noted that this one exception is sufficient to bring into question the necessity of the days of Genesis 1 being twenty-four-hour days on the basis of their appearance with

[143] The singular term *yôm* occurs with the cardinal number "one" in Genesis 1:5; 27:45; 33:13; Numbers 11:19; 1 Samuel 9:15; 27:1.

[144] Bruce K. Waltke, "The Literary Genre of Genesis, Chapter 1," 7.

[145] Gleason L. Archer, *Encyclopedia of Bible Difficulties,* Zondervan, 1982, pp. 59–61.

ordinal numbers in that context.[146] Because of Geisler's suggestion, it is appropriate to address his claim.

This one exception may occur in Hosea 6:2, a clearly poetic expression of the ANE numerical parallelism formula x//x+1.[147] Examples of this conventional ancient Near Eastern literary device can be seen in poetic passages such as Job 40:5; Proverbs 6:16–19; 30:15, 18, 21, 29; Amos 1:3, 6, 9, and numerous others.[148] This poetic prophecy in Hosea 6:2 may or may not provide an exception to the rule: "From two days (*yōmayim*: dual form of *yôm*) He will restore us, on the third day (*bayyôm haššᵉlîšî*), He will raise us, that we may live before Him." If this verse is a prophecy of the resurrection of Christ, which some hold, twenty-four-hour days are still in view, and Hosea 6:2 is not an exception to the rule.[149] If a national restoration of Israel is in view instead, it may be of indefinite stated length, but of finite duration. In other words, the restoration will *one day* be complete (pardon the paronomasia). On the other hand, being employed as a conventional poetical x/x+1 device, the occurrence in Hosea 6:2 is probably not relevant in the discussion of the meaning of *yôm* in this passage because Genesis 1 is narrative rather than poetry. Too, x//x+1 parallelism does not exist in Genesis 1 nor anywhere else in biblical Hebrew narrative texts, but only in poetic and prophetic texts.[150] Unless Genesis 1 is to be understood as an entirely different and special type of creation genre (and again, there is no current archaeological or inscriptional support

---

[146] Norman L. Geisler, *Baker Encyclopedia of Christian Apologetics*, Zondervan, 1999, 271.

[147] For more on this literary convention of the ANE world, see Wolfgang M. W. Roth, "The Numerical Sequence x/x+1 in the Old Testament," *Vetus Testamentum* 12 (1962): 300–311.

[148] A variant form x//10x occurs in 1 Samuel. 18:7; 21:11, and elsewhere.

[149] Support for understanding Hosea 6:2 as referring to the resurrection of Christ may be derived from the words of the apostle Paul in 1 Corinthians 15:4: "that he was raised again on the third day according to the Scriptures" (NIV). Nowhere else in the OT might predict the timing of the resurrection. Arguing against this viewpoint would be the thinking of some that Paul had in mind the gospel predictions of Christ's resurrection (Mark 14:58 and John 2:19, 21).

[150] There are brief poetic sections in narrative passages that do contain the similar x/10x numerical parallelism, such as in 1 Samuel 18:7.

for this conjecture) rather than straightforward Hebrew narrative, the term *yôm* with ordinals indicates twenty-four-hour days there as well.[151]

As a Temporal Adverb (*b^e yôm* plus infinitive construct)

Though not technically in the initial creation pericope (a literary section), the term *yôm* does appear proximately in 2:4b with the inseparable preposition *bêt* just before the infinitive construct *ʿăśôṯ* ("to make"). It is now thought by many scholars that this construction is a Hebrew idiom that probably should be understood as an indefinite temporal adverb and translated "when the LORD God made. . . ."[152] Thus the NIV translates it as "when" in Genesis 2:4 as well as several other places in Genesis (2:17; 3:5; 5:1, 2). If this construction is to be understood as an idiomatic usage, then such occurrences add nothing to the argument one way or the other.

Conclusion of the Use of *yôm* in Genesis 1:1–2:3

The most glaring omission within Genesis 1:1–2:3 is the use of *yôm* in the construct (or, bound) relationship. Outside of Genesis 1, there are numerous examples of *yôm* in construct with other nouns which may indicate indefinite lengths of time. Such examples of this construct relationship would include the "day of battle" (1 Sam. 13:22; Job 38:23), the "day of calamity" (Deut. 32:35; Prov. 27:10), the "day of vengeance" (Prov. 6:23; Isa. 34:8), the "day of prosperity" (Eccl. 7:14), the "day of gladness of heart" (Cant. 3:11 = Wedding

---

[151] It may well be that some ANE passage more directly parallel to the Genesis 1 account may someday be revealed by the turning of the spade or in the rubble of the *gufa* bucket. Such new input may affirm or deny my position. Until that occurs, however, one must accept the overwhelming data offered by like usage elsewhere in Scripture as paramount.

[152] Cf. the translation of this word in Genesis 2:4b in Waltke and O'Connor, *An Introduction to Biblical Hebrew Syntax*,(Eisenbraun's, 1990): 250, 611; David M. Fouts, "Response Two to 'How Long an Evening and Morning,'" *Creation Ex Nihilo Technical Journal* 11:3 (1997): 303–4; and "How Short an Evening and Morning?" *CENTech Journal* 11:3 (1997): 307–8. It was perhaps, that because he did not recognize this idiom, St. Augustine argued that the creation had all occurred in a moment of time.

Day [or week?]), "day of the Lord" (Joel 1:15; 2:1, numerous others),[153] the "day of salvation" (Isa. 49:8). Using the plural, examples include: "the days of the Philistines," "the days of Noah," "the days of Uzziah," "the days of Ahasuerus," "the days of Josiah," etc. Yet, some appeal to this very syntactical structure, *which is not to be found anywhere in Genesis 1:1–2:3,* to argue that *yôm* has in our passage the potential meaning of an indefinite day of millions or billions of years in length![154]

When one considers the usages of *yôm* in very similar grammatical and syntactical contexts elsewhere in the Old Testament Hebrew text, it appears that *yôm* cannot be understood as an indefinite and lengthy period of time in any of its usages in Genesis 1:1–2:3. Since the term does not exist in our Genesis 1:1–2:3 pericope in the "construct" state with any other word, appeals to other construct usages outside of 1:1–2:3 to demonstrate how *yôm* could be used indefinitely are specious. In fact, "day" and "days" are never used elsewhere in the Hebrew Bible in any syntactical construction in the sense of multiple thousands or millions of years, i.e., the period of time necessary for evolution to have occurred. This is true even if one sees indefinite periods of time where *yôm* is used in construct with other nouns, ***which situation does not occur in Genesis 1***. The burden of proof rests upon those who would argue differently—scriptural usage does not allow for such nuances.

Excursus: Evening and Morning (*wayᵉhî ʿereb̲ wayᵉhî b̲ōqer*)

[153] The term "day of the Lord" is a theologically technical term with past, present, or future aspects of blessing or judgment depending on the context in which it is found. The length of time involved varies according to God's purposes.

[154] Cf. Hugh Ross, *The Fingerprint of God*, 146; *A Matter of Days*, 11. Ross uses "millions of years" for a possible understanding of *yôm*. I do not recall having read that he would elevate this to billions of years.

A phrase offered repeatedly in Genesis 1 is "and there was evening and there was morning, day x" (*wayᵉhî ʿereḇ wayᵉhî ḇōqer, yôm* x). This syntactical phrase (employing *wayᵉhî* before each noun) is unique, occurring only in Genesis 1. The similar expression placing "morning" before "evening" is more prevalent in other parts of Scripture where it normally indicates regular daytime activities, such as the sacrifices offered morning and evening (2 Chron. 2:4; Ex. 18:13). When "evening" precedes "morning" outside of Genesis 1, such as in Exodus 27:21 and Leviticus 24:3, it refers to a nightly task (such as keeping the lamps burning in the tabernacle). In Numbers 19:21, evening is used with reference to the cloud of God's presence (which appeared as fire: Num. 19:15) overshadowing the tabernacle overnight. Thus it seems that the particular order of evening before morning in Genesis 1 could simply be indicating the period of darkness following the daylight activity of the creative hand of God (a decree followed by fulfillment and assessment: see discussion below).

On the other hand, the phrase "evening and morning" can also indicate a single twenty-four-hour day. This may be illustrated in Daniel 8, where the term "evening" precedes "morning" asyndetically[155] twice. In Daniel 8:14, the terms are qualified by the numerical modifier twenty-three hundred (2,300). The KJV renders this phrase as twenty-three hundred days, and there is no valid reason, even in prophetic literature, to read it differently. In fact, counted days are common in Daniel's prophetic messages. For instance, in Daniel 12, verse 11 contains the phrase twelve –hundred-ninety (1,290) days, and verse 12 reveals thirteen-hundred-thirty-five (1,335) days. Now certainly one may concede that in any of these cases in Daniel the numbers could have symbolic meaning. Any symbolic meaning

[155] "Asyndetically" means without the connective "and." The text here simply reads "*ʿereḇ bōqer*."

of the numbers in Daniel 12 does not automatically preclude the normal meaning of *yôm*, however, and should not automatically preclude the normal meaning of "evening morning" used in 8:14. Assuming for the sake of argument that the entire phrase is symbolic, then what is the symbol? What does "twenty-three hundred evening/morning" represent? The book of Daniel is very good with explaining both dreams (chs. 2, 4) and visions (chs. 5, 7, 8, 9), but there are no explanations immediately offered for these specific words in 8:14, which seems to indicate that none were needed because they are to be understood literally.[156] The mention of *ʿereḇ bōqer* in 8:14 then serves as the antecedent reference for the mention of the same in 8:26, wherein Gabriel explains to Daniel the certainty of the fulfillment of the vision of the evenings and mornings.[157] Time passage as we would understand it certainly seems to be in view in both of these verses in this passage. But once again, if it were symbolic in the prophecy of Daniel (and I don't think it is), then to argue that the symbol involves an indefinite amount of time is a conclusion foisted on the text from outside, and there is no such indication in Daniel. To then apply such an interpretation of Daniel's usage of *ʿereḇ bōqer* in prophetic literature as indefinite time inferring millions of years to the historical narrative of Genesis 1:1–2:3 is at best special pleading, at worst untenable.

Since evening and morning are understood and used literally in the vast majority of cases as "evening and morning" in the Hebrew Bible, there is no evidence to indicate they should have a differing meaning in Genesis 1. Either ordering of the words, evening first or morning first, seems to indicate a time passage of no more than twenty-four-hours. In fact,

[156] If prophetic, which I hold it to be, the words may have had an actual fulfillment from the time of the desecration of the temple by Antiochus IV Epiphanes between ca. 171 BC and 165 BC, and the Maccabean act of re-consecrating the desecrated temple ca. 165 BC. If historical, an *ex eventu* reference to the same occurrence would also necessitate a literal twenty-three hundred days.

[157] The entire argument of Isaiah 40–48 is that the Lord is the only god who can predict and effect the future, even to the naming of a ruler (Cyrus) prior to his birth. A prediction of specific lengths of time should be no problem for Him.

the unusual construction of *way^ehî ʿereḇ way^ehî ḇōqer* "and there was evening and there was morning, day x" in Genesis 1 must mean one twenty-four-hour day, since it stands in each instance in apposition to "day x" or "xth day," which also must be a twenty-four-hour day. That is to say, the phrases are to be understood as equal in value, elegant in expression.

Excursus: Statement of Completion: And it Was So (*way^ehî kēn*)[158]

The use of *kēn,* "thus, so,"[159] is found frequently in the Hebrew Scriptures. This word, prefaced by the preterite form of "to be" (*wayhî* or *way^ehî* depending on accentuation) is found in Genesis 1:7, 9, 11, 15, 24, 30 (i.e., at the end of the initial creative decrees of God on days 2, 3, 4 and 6). It occurs exactly as *way^ehî kēn* only twice elsewhere biblically.[160] In Judges 6:38, it refers to the completion of Gideon's first test with the fleece. It thus must be seen as reflecting the accomplishment of a task. The second occurrence of the phrase in found in 2 Kings 15:12. In that passage, the prophecy spoken to Jehu concerning his royal lineage issued in 2 Kings 10:30 is said to have been fulfilled by the kingship of Zechariah. This fulfillment is registered by the phrase *way^ehî kēn.* Though these two examples do not provide absolutely conclusive evidence, they are the only two uses of the exact phrase outside of Genesis 1. A consistent adherent to the verbal, plenary inspiration of Scripture should at least consider the testimony they offer that something has been completed when the identical constructions are found in Genesis 1. This means that the decrees issued by God on a given day were all carried out within the same twenty-four-hour period in which He issued His decree.

---

[158] It is thought by some that the phrase "and there was light" (*way^ehî ʾôr*) in 1:3 serves as a statement of completion similar to *way^ehî kēn.* Cf. Ronald Hendel, *The Text of Genesis 1–11*, (Oxford, 1998): 20.

[159] "Yes" in modern Hebrew.

[160] Further study into the textual analysis of this phrase in both the MT and LXX can be found in Hendel, 20–23.

Seven: The Creation Week Continues Genesis 1:6–8

We are told in Genesis 1:6–8 that on the second day the Lord God created a division in the waters, separating the waters into two locations. The waters under this "expanse" were called "seas" and the waters above it were called "heavens." The term used for "expanse" (NASV) in the Hebrew Bible is the term *rāqîa'* .[161] It was translated as "firmament" in the KJV, a gloss that has subsequently led many to understand the words to convey the meaning of a solid dome over the earth. Add to this the fact that many ancient cultures may have so regarded the heavens as well, long before the KJV of 1611, and then there is plenty of foundation for misunderstanding what the text is actually saying.

The term *rāqîa'* occurs seventeen times in the Hebrew Old Testament, and five of them are in the three verses under consideration here, with four more found elsewhere in chapter 1. To be sure, *rāqîa'* is the nominal form of the verb *rāqa'* (used 12x), which BDB says means basically to "beat, stamp, beat out, stretch out."[162] I shall now offer some examples. This verb describes the activities of metal workers hammering out (spreading out or stretching) gold to make the ephod for the high priest (Ex. 39:3). The same process is used to hammer out bronze to make plating for the altar (Num. 16:39 [MT 17:3–4]). The prophet Isaiah describes the similar work of a goldsmith overlaying a wooden idol with beaten-out gold, a process of spreading the gold over a framework (Isa. 44:12; cf. the similar use of Jer.

---

[161] The Greek of the LXX is interestingly enough the term *stereōma*, the word from which we get our English term "stereo." Perhaps its use here is focusing on the two directions.: above and below.

[162] BDB, 956.

10:9). In Ezekiel 25:6, the verb is used to illustrate the nation of Ammon stamping its foot in glee over the destruction of Judah by the Babylonians (cf. similar use in Ezek. 6:11). Otherwise the verb is used to describe God's activities at the creation and thus may shed light on the nominal form in that context. Job 37:18 asks: "Can you spread out the sky with Him?" Psalm 136:6 claims that He spread out the earth over the waters. Isaiah 42:5 and 44:24 parallel the verb *rāqa'* synonymously with the Hebrew verb *nāṭâ*, which means to "spread out, pitch a tent." In these two cases, the heavens are spread out like a tent, and the earth is spread out like hammered metal over the seas.

But it is not the verbal form *rāqa'* that is found in Genesis 1. Instead, it is the nominal form *rāqîa'*. In another context, *rāqîa'* synonymously parallels the term "heavens": "The heavens are recounting the glory of God, and the expanse is declaring the work of His hands" (Ps. 19:1; Dan. 12:3 is similar). The rendering in Genesis 1: 14, 15, 17, and 20 of "the expanse of heaven" therefore seems to be a genitive of description, and may be translated as "the heavenly expanse"; or as a genitive of apposition, translated as "the expanse which is heaven." This latter seems to be the best understanding in light of Genesis 1:8: "God named the *rāqîa'* heaven." This expanse (or, the heavens) in Genesis 1 was able to contain the birds on wing, the sun, moon, planets, and stars as well (1:14, 17, 20).[163] So it seems from this short study that God spread out the heavens like a tent, or spread them out in the manner of a worker beating out his metal to fit his mold. It probably therefore was not intended to convey the idea of a hardened and impenetrable dome but rather something stretched out with

---

[163] In Ezekiel's initial vision, there is a vast expanse appearing above the throne of God (1:22, 23, 25, 26; cf. 10:1).

purpose and design, which could contain both life (birds) and luminaries (sun, moon, stars, planets).[164]

The first day of the creation week had not been referred to as "first day" but rather as "day one" *yôm 'eḥaḏ*. This is the one use of *yôm* in 1:1–2:3 that occurs with the cardinal number as opposed to the ordinals associated with *yôm* on subsequent days. Though the Hebrews had numerous ways of designating "first," there was no need to do so prior to there being a "second." In other words, if one is all there is, it doesn't require the designation of "first." Hence, simply "day one" is found in the text. Subsequent days, such as the second day in 1:8, are described by the ordinal numbers, as well as being in apposition to the phrase "and there was evening and there was morning," which means essentially a twenty-four-hour day as shown above.

Four out of the six days so ordered by the ordinal numbers (second through fifth days) occur without the benefit of an article "the" on either the noun *yôm* or the qualifying ordinal number, which fact has led some to see the days of creation as being indefinite, with the ordering of the days being more literary than literal. In other words, the fact that the second through fifth days have no "the" indicates to some that one should not expect to find a literal ordering of the days of creation. The implication of this understanding is that one need not see the creation account's ordering of days as having any real time significance at all. The six creative days would then instead simply be an artistic way of describing the magnificent work of God, in no particular order. This issue demands some special attention.

---

[164] There has been much discussion over ancient artistic depictions of the "expanse," which seem to indicate an actual ocean of waters above the "expanse," or at times, a hardened dome, either of which contains the atmospheric heavens and the heavenly bodies as well. The present writer prefers to understand the text differently at this point, since the text leaves unclear the meaning of the "waters above," calling only the waters below the "seas." Too, the meaning of *rāqîa'* does not demand a hardened surface of any kind.

The Ordinal Numbers of Genesis 1

When one observes an English text of Genesis 1, it becomes readily apparent that many editors inserted a definite article onto the ordinal numbers in their translations in order to read "the second day," "the third day," etc. (KJV, NIV, NAB). At a recent discussion on creationism in 2004 and again at the national ETS meetings in 2007, another Old Testament scholar took issue with this traditional rendering, questioning the validity of inserting the English article "the" into the translation, inasmuch as the second through fifth days are in Hebrew anarthrous; that is, there is no article ("the") present with either the noun or the modifying ordinal number.[165] ("The" in Hebrew is normally expressed morphologically by the prefix *ha* plus doubling of the next consonant.) If the suggestion made by the other professor should stand, then one may feel free, as he does, to render the phrases as "a second day," "a third day" (NASV, RSV) and so forth. As an example, to so render simply "second day" or "a second day" would allow this described in Genesis 1 to refer to any one of many possible days in a period of time of unspecified length, or to *represent* a typical day in this stage of creation, or even to represent *a* stage in creation, even without regard to the order of creation. So "There was evening and there was morning, a second day" may mean "There was evening and morning, a day in the second period of creation" or "There was evening and morning, a second day [or period of creation]" or "There was evening and morning, another day of creation."

---

[165] Ronald Youngblood, "The Days of Genesis 1: Anarthrous and Chronological/Nonchronological," oral presentation at the Evangelical Theological Society, San Diego, Nov. 2007. Youngblood, in emphasizing the anarthrous ordinals, seems to be arguing the Framework hypothesis, which sees 1:1–2:3 as being literary, rather than literal, and thus having little to no value in the debate regarding the date of the creation. Though I disagree with the Framework hypothesis, I applaud Youngblood's careful attention to the morphology of the canonical text.

Should this be our understanding? It is necessary at this juncture to demonstrate that the proper understanding of the passage at hand would expect a translation of the phrases as definite, rather than indefinite. In other words, one should render the phrases as "the fourth day," "the fifth day," rather than "a fourth day," "a fifth day," etc. This assertion is supported by the fact that in biblical Hebrew definiteness is determined in a number of different ways, only one of which involves the use of the article *ha* plus doubling of the next consonant.[166] It is therefore necessary to examine these usages before applying the results to our study of Genesis 1.

Different Ways to Show Definiteness in Biblical Hebrew

The Use of the Article

One of the most common ways of expressing definiteness is to simply prefix *ha–* plus doubling of the next consonant of a given noun. For instance, *sûs* ("a horse") becomes *hassûs* ("the horse"), *melek* ("a king") becomes *hammelek* ("the king"). Though there are some morphological and phonological variants to this basic method, the presence of the article indicates definiteness or specificity (*yôm* > *hayyôm* standing alone can mean "the day," "this day," or "today" depending on the context).

Proper Nouns

Proper nouns (those which name people or places, such as our English terms Dennis Ingolfsland or Saginaw, Michigan) are understood in biblical Hebrew to be definite without the benefit of having the prefixed *ha* plus doubling.[167]

---

[166] For the first-year Hebrew student, the *pataḥ* vowel of the definite article may at times lengthen to a *qāmeṣ* to compensate for first guttural nouns.

[167] There are examples in the Hebrew text where even proper nouns are so prefixed, but this is done for emphasis (analogous to "Am I speaking to *the* Andrew Snelling?" in English).

Nouns in Construct with Other Nouns

Another way that definiteness is indicated in biblical Hebrew is by means of the construct (or bound) relationship. As was discussed above, this involves the very close association of two or more nouns juxtaposed in order to indicate a genitival ("of *something*") relationship. In such cases, the first of the two nouns (called the "construct") is normally found anarthrous (without the article) but may be understood as definite if the second of the chain (called the "absolute") is definite or understood to be definite. An example would be *sûs hammelek* "the horse of the king." Even though *sûs* is without a definite article, since the absolute term *melek* has a definite article, *sûs* is translated as if it had a definite article. Another example would be *bêṯ dāwîd*, which is translated "the house of David," because although the absolute term is without a definite article, it is *understood* to be definite because David is a proper noun. A third situation would be an instance where the absolute term is associated with a possessive pronoun. An example of this would be *sûs malkô*, which is translated "the horse of his king" because the absolute term is described by the suffixed pronoun "his." In the last two situations the definite article is absent, yet both nouns are very definite and specific.

Pronominal Suffixes

Because the presence of a pronominal suffix on a noun establishes a bound construct relationship between the noun and its suffix, the noun is definite even though lacking a definite article (*i.e.* though morphologically anarthrous). For instance the juxtaposition of the term *melek* and the pronominal suffix for "me" or "my" (*–î*) yields *malkî* "my king" or literally "the king of mine."[168] No article is necessary to establish definiteness.

The Nature of Ordinal Sequencing

Sequencing of events or people seems to be the reason that ordinal numbers exist in any language. This includes biblical Hebrew. There are numerous examples of ordinal numbers sequencing events and people. But there are no examples of which I am aware that demonstrate a literary rather than literal understanding. For example, to claim that the term "a second son" refers to, let's say, "the second son we'll deal with here in the text" or "the second son I recall to mind" rather than "the second son born to his father" seems to be literarily distinct from an ordered list such as we find in Genesis 1. Waltke says: "The ordinals express degree, quality, or position in a series."[169] Since the purpose of ordinals is to establish sequencing in a narrative text (or in an oral proclamation for that matter), they are in and of themselves specific and definite. Otherwise they have little meaning of practical value.

So, to argue for an *indefinite* understanding of the phrases in Genesis 1 based on the anarthrous ordinal numbers with a view to supporting a literary rather than literal interpretation is tenuous at best, as there is enough evidence to indicate definiteness within the immediate context of Genesis 1 without the use of the definite article.

Application to Genesis 1

In the following discussion, only the second through fifth days are in view. The first day in Hebrew is *yôm 'eḥād*, employing a cardinal rather than an ordinal. The sixth day is

[168] For the Hebrew student: segholate nouns revert to their proto–Semitic forms before adding suffixes, hence a suffixed *melek* reverts to the earlier form *malk–* before suffixing.
[169] Waltke, *Syntax*, 272.

somewhat anomalous, and will be dealt with below the discussion of the anarthrous ordinals. The seventh "day" is articular (having the article "the"); hence the modifying ordinal "seventh" also has the article by normal grammatical agreement.[170]

According to the excellent Hebrew concordance by Even–Shoshan, one notes that the ordinals "second" through "fifth" are sometimes articular in other parts of the Hebrew Bible, because the modified noun has the article or is definite by one of the means mentioned above. This is called grammatical agreement. On the other hand, at times the ordinal in Scripture is anarthrous, because the modified noun does not have the article. The determining factor is found in the presence or absence of the article in the nouns that are modified. My contention is that the presence of the ordinal number itself is sufficient to establish the definiteness of the noun modified, regardless of the presence or absence of an article on that noun or on the ordinal number that describes it. The following discussion should explain my reasons.

The ordinal "second" (*šēnî*) occurs anarthrously (without the article) ten times, and over 110 times with the article. The ten occurrences are worthy of mention. Besides here in Genesis 1:8, "second" occurs also in Numbers 8:8 (a second bull taken for a sin offering); 2 Kings 9:19 (a second horseman sent to Jehu); Ecclesiastes. 4:8 (a descendent is implied); Ecclesiastes 4:10 (a second person); Esther 2:14 ("second" modifies "house of women"); Nehemiah 3:30 (the repair of a second section of wall in sequence from a given gate); 1 Chronicles 3:1 (the second son of David). Though some might argue for a translation in these cases to be simply "another," all of these examples demonstrate in their context the

---

170 "Ordinals agree in gender with the nouns they modify" (Allen P. Ross, *Introducing Biblical Hebrew*, (Baker, 2001): 182). "The ordinals express degree, quality, or position in a series, 'first, second, third'; in Hebrew these are adjectives" (Bruce K. Waltke and M. O'Connor, *Syntax*, 272). The ordinal "sixth" occurs anarthrously only in Genesis 30:19 with reference to the Zebulon, the sixth son born to Leah and Jacob. The ordinals "seventh," "eighth," and "ninth" are always articular throughout the Old Testament.

definiteness and importance of the second person, group, or event even though they are morphologically anarthrous (again, without the article) in the text.[171]

There are two occurrences of "second" without an article, which are worthy of note in Genesis 30:7 (a second son for Jacob from Bilhah: Naphtali), and in Genesis 30:12 (a second son for Jacob from Zilpah: Asher). In each of these cases, the term seems to indicate simply "another" inasmuch as strict ordering of birth would have placed Naphtali as the sixth son of Jacob and Asher as the eighth. However, in each case the text does not order the sons with Jacob in view, but their mothers, the handmaidens Bilhah and Zilpah. So whereas one reading the text may claim "another son" for Jacob, the meaning of "the second son" is more accurate to the context. In the same way, one may simply say that since "second day" in Genesis 1:8 has no article to insure definiteness, it could be understood as simply "another day" of creation. This is unlikely for two reasons: One must take into context the fact that Genesis 1 is an account of daily events in the creation week and that the term "second day" occurs within that context with the other ordinals third, fourth, fifth, sixth, and seventh. Also, although one may ascribe a generic "another" to other occurrences of anarthrous "seconds" found in Scripture, one does not employ that nuance for "a third" or "a fourth" or "a fifth," which are also found in the passage under study.

"Second" occurs with the article and modifies *yôm* in Exodus 2:13; Numbers 7:18; 29:17; Joshua 6:14; 10:32; Judges 20:24, 25; Jeremiah 41:4; Ezekiel 43:22; Esther 7:2; and Nehemiah 8:13. In each of these cases, the term *yôm* is prefixed with the preposition *b–* with the *a*–vowel indicating the article,[172] necessitating by grammatical agreement the presence of

[171] Only in Numbers 8:8 might it be construed that a second bull could be taken out of sequence, but given the strict ritual of sacrifice normally understood in the cultic practices of Israel, so construing it would be regarded as special pleading.
[172] For the first-year Hebrew student, the *hē* of the article is replaced by the *bêt* preposition in these cases.

the article on "second." All of these instances are sequencing time, and referencing a specific day. These examples all show the normal understanding of the ordinal "second" found with the word "day."

The ordinal "third" (*šᵉlîšî*) occurs only twice without the article; here in Genesis 1:13 and in Deuteronomy 23:9 (23:8 English). In the latter case, it refers to the third generation of converted Edomites or Egyptians who are able to be numbered among the assembly of Israel. This is not simply "a third generation" as a strict observation of the anarthrous form might suggest to some, but that which is sequenced after the first and second, i.e., the generation that would soonest be allowed to participate in the Israelite worship. The absence of the article is irrelevant to the discussion in this context and does not nullify definiteness.

There are thirty occurrences of the term "third" with the article present where the ordinal modifies *yôm*. In passages where this tandem occurs, the normal expression often involves a preposition: "on the third day" (Genesis 22:4; 2 Chron. 10:12). One would therefore expect the modifying ordinal to also be articular in keeping with grammatical agreement of a noun with modifying attributive adjective. In each of the cases, time is sequenced, and each time is definite and specific.

The term "fourth" (*rᵉḇîʿî*) appears anarthrously only twice in the MT, both in Genesis (1:19; 15:16). In the latter case, it refers to the fourth generation of Israel that will return to the land after the sojourn in Egypt. A specific and definite generation is in view and the ordinal is sufficient to explain this, therefore there is no need for the article.

Used with the article, "fourth" also occurs modifying *yôm*. In each of these cases, the *bêt* preposition again governs the noun ("on the fourth day"), which is modified by the articular ordinal that sequences time (Numb. 7:30, 29:23; Judg. 19:5; Ezra 8:33; 2 Chron. 20:26).

The ordinal "fifth" (*ḥămîšî*) occurs without the definite article only twice in the MT, both in Genesis (1:23; 30:17). The latter case refers to Issachar, the fifth son of Leah and Jacob. Definiteness and specificity are not determined by the article, which is absent, rather by the ordinal itself, which indicates the position of Issachar in the family that is defined as "Leah and Jacob" and not as "Jacob and all his wives." So though Issachar was the ninth listed son of Jacob with respect to all of his wives/concubines, he was the fifth son of Leah and Jacob specifically. There is no need for an article to explain this.

Used with the article, "fifth" occurs over thirty times. Three of these occurrences involve modifying *yôm.* Numbers 7:36 involves the order of tribal sacrifice offered "on the fifth day." Numbers 29:26 refers to the order of sacrifices offered during the fifth day of the feast of trumpets. In Judges 19:8, the Levite attempts to leave his father–in–law yet once again "on the fifth day."

In all these examples, both of anarthrous ordinal numbers and articular ordinals used with "day," one may draw some conclusions. First, and with very few exceptions, anarthrous ordinals are still definite within their contexts. This means that in Genesis 1 one should also understand them as definite, especially as they appear in an ordered list. Second, when found modifying "day," my study has found that the resulting constructions within their contexts always refer to activities on or within a given twenty-four-hour day, no matter if the article is present or not.

Youngblood's Appeal to ANE Texts

In his recent ETS presentation, Ron Youngblood tried to make a case for reading the anarthrous ordinals of Genesis 1 as literary rather than literal. In part, he appealed to four Ugaritic texts (CTA 4:vi; 14:ii–iii (two examples); CTA 17:i) and tablet XI of the Gilgamesh epic.[173] English translations of these texts are repeated here for comparison sake.

> Fire was set in the mansion, flames in the palace.
> Behold! A day and a second the fire consumed in the mansion,
> the flames in the palace.
> A third, a fourth day the fire consumed in the mansion,
> the flames in the palace.
> A fifth, a sixth day the fire consumed [in] the mansion,
> the flames in [the midst of the] palace.
> Then on the seventh day the fire escaped from the mansion,
> The flames from the palace.
> The silver had turned into plates,
> The gold had been turned into bricks.
> Mightiest Baal did rejoice, (saying):
> "I have built my mansion of silver,
> My palace of Gold."[174]

> Let them settle like locusts on the field,
> like hoppers on the fringe of the wilderness.
> Go a day and a second,
> a third, a fourth day,
> a fifth, a sixth day;
> then with the sun on the seventh (day)
> you shall come to great Udm,
> and to well–watered Udm;
> and do you tarry at the city,
> encamp at the town.[175]

> Stay quiet a day and a second,
> a third, a fourth day,
> a fifth, a sixth day;
> do not discharge your arrows into the town
> (nor) your sling stones (into) the citadel.
> And behold! with the sun on the seventh (day),
> then king Pabil will not sleep,

[173] Youngblood, "The Days of Genesis 1," oral presentation at 2007 ETS.

[174] CTA 4:vi, *ll.* 22–38. The designation CTA is the standard reference for Andrée Herdner, *Corpus des tablettes en cunéiformes alphabétiques,* Paris: Paul Guenther, 1963. The English translations cited here are from J. C. L. Gibson, *Canaanite Myths and Legends*, T&T Clark, 1977.

[175] CTA 14:ii–iii, *ll.* 104–111.

for the rumbling of the roaring of his bull(s)
for the sound of the braying of his ass(es),
for the lowing of the plough ox(en),
the whining of his hunting dog(s).[176]

Behold! A day [and a second]
Daniel (gave) the gods [. . . . .],[177]
He gave [the gods . . . . .] to eat,
[he gave] the holy ones . . . . . [to drink].
A third, a fourth day
Daniel (gave) the gods [. . . . .],
[he] gave [the gods] . . . . . to eat,
He gave the [holy ones] . . . . . to drink.
A fifth day, a sixth day
Daniel (gave)[the gods] . . . . . ,
He gave the gods . . . . . to eat,
He gave the holy ones [. . . . .] to drink.
Daniel put aside his cloak,
He put aside his cloak, he ascended and lay down,
[he put aside] his loincloth, and so he passed the night.
Then on the seventh day
Baal drew near with his supplication:
'The misery of Daniel, man of Rapiu!'[178]

On Mount Nimuš the boat ran aground,
Mount Nimuš held the boat fast and did not let it move.
One day, a second day, Mount Nimuš held the boat fast and did not let it move,
A third day, a fourth day, Mount Nimuš held the boat fast and did not let it move,
A fifth, a sixth, Mount Nimuš held the boat fast and did not let it move.
When the seventh day arrived—
I brought out a dove, setting it free:[179]

In each of these texts, the sequencing of ordinals first through seventh is used, each modifying an Akkadian or Ugaritic cognate of the Hebrew *yôm*, and all appear anarthrously.

---

[176] CTA 14:iii, *ll.* 114–123.
[177] The ellipsis indicates a lacunae (damaged or missing word/words) in extant ancient texts.
[178] CTA 17:i, *ll.* 6–18. The Daniel mentioned here is not to be confused with the Daniel of the Bible. The former, more properly Dan'el since there is no equivalent to the *yôd* in the Ugaritic orthography of the word to represent the vowel "i." Too, the Dan'el of Ugaritic myth was a heavy drinker, an adulterer, and an idol worshipper; hardly worthy of comparison with the righteous Daniel (cf. Ezek. 14:14).
[179] A. R. George, *The Babylonian Gilgamesh Epic: Introduction, Critical Edition and Cuneiform Texts* (Oxford, University Press, 2003): tablet xi, *ll.* 142–148.

In none of these texts is the creation in view but rather the building of Baal's palace, the plans of an attacking army, sacrifices to a god, and a poetic Babylonian flood account. In Youngblood's opinion, since the ordinals are anarthrous in these texts, they may not be understood to be definite or specific. Drawing parallels with the text of Genesis, he concludes that the biblical text therefore may also be understood as indefinitely numbered days; as literary, not literal, and built upon a framework founded on the terms *tōhû wāḇōhû* in 1:2. In this so–called Framework hypothesis, days one to three complete the unformed part (*tōhû*) and days four to six complete the unfilled part (*ḇōhû*). In so doing, Youngblood also names the sun as having been created on day one, rather than on the fourth day as the biblical text says.[180]

In response to Youngblood's position, since the Ugaritic and Babylonian languages apparently lack a definite article (i.e., all nouns in Ugaritic and Akkadian are anarthrous), his point may be moot as the languages are not sufficiently similar to Hebrew in this regard. In other words, it is hard to argue one way or another about poetic texts in other languages that don't ever employ any definite articles in discussing the use or non-use of definite articles on ordinal numbers in the narrative Genesis 1 context.

Furthermore, one will notice that, though they employ ordinal numbers modifying the word "day," the texts cited above do so differently than the Scripture does. They offer little in the way of differing actions occurring on the sequential days (fire continues to consume, the troops wait in patience, Dan'el offers food and drink to the gods daily, Mt. Nimus will not release the boat), whereas the Scripture relates the differing commands of God in orderly sequence as He creates the heavens and the earth and all that they contain (cf. Ex. 20:11).

---

[180] Youngblood, "The Days of Genesis 1."

Too, the Ugaritic texts he cites are clearly epic poetry, more closely related to the genre of the Bible's own Psalms than they are to the narrative texts of the Pentateuch. The Gilgamesh epic is an epic poetic account of an ancient flood account similar to the Bible's narrative accounts of Noah's Flood. Though the language and literature of other ANE cultures is certainly important to shed light on the scriptural texts (and I think, certainly more important than the findings of science in the discussion of Genesis 1 because the ANE texts are more closely related), they cannot sit as judge over it. Therefore, since epic extrabiblical poetry is not historical narrative of the Bible, it can only be used for illustrative purposes, not for final interpretation.

Finally, though light can exist apart from the sun, as it will in the future as described by Revelation 21:23, for one to claim that the creation of the sun occurred on day one and not the fourth day divests the creation passage of any meaning whatsoever. "A fourth day" cannot be "day one" without some clear indication in the text which overrides the otherwise clear natural reading of the text. Such a clear indication does not exist in Genesis 1.

Conclusion

Why then do the ordinals second through fifth occur without the definite article in Genesis 1? The answer may exist in the fact that *yôm* itself has no article in these cases, so there is no need for grammatical agreement in the ordinals. Another plausible answer may be found in the thought conveyed by the text itself, that there were no other second (or third or fourth or fifth) days of the week yet that would cause confusion by the absence of the article. In other words, the only possible meaning of "a second day" in that context is definite and specific because it is not day one. It exists in an orderly list. It is the next day in the progression. The same is true for the third, fourth, and fifth days. Too, the fact is that in each of these cases, the phrases "a second day," "a third day," and the others occur in apposition to the unique and specific phrase "and there was evening and there was morning" which phrase completes the cycle of command, fulfillment, and assessment of the activities of that day. *In a highly stylized narrative, the phrases, anarthrous yet definite, offer a repetitive and easily memorized orderly sequencing of the events of the creation week.* Each day is specific, definite, and unique. To assume that they are numbered sequentially irrespective of their actual order destroys the normally understood function and purpose of ordinal numbers.

Eight: The Third, Fourth, and Fifth Days of Creation Genesis 1:9–23

The third day of creation brings a number of significant data to bear on the discussion. One issue is the separation of the waters below into seas as distinct from the dry land, upon which the vegetation would grow. There is not a lot of detail given here in the text, but simply that the jussive of command is again given by God with the resulting consequence and assessment. In this case perhaps, nothing new was created but rather only an organization of that which existed as the day began. Certainly this is true for the waters of the seas that, existing before day one, had just yesterday (on the second day) been separated from the waters above. It may also be similarly understood for the earth, here named as dry land as distinct from the waters of the seas, as it simply was commanded to "appear." Assuming for a moment that the state of the earth in 1:2 was a water-covered sphere, then this act on day three would have involved some further physical changes. Whether those changes involved the lowering of the seas or the raising of the land mass or a combination of both is not detailed here. Any of these is possible, perhaps by tectonic activity such as subduction of plates. Geologists may wish to consider this when forming their hypotheses.

There are many who suggest that establishing vegetation on the earth could not have been fully accomplished within one day, especially as the text seems to indicate that mature trees were created on that day. How could this be? In years past, many of us have seen examples of "time–lapse" photography, wherein hours or days are reduced to mere moments, say in the budding and blooming of a rose. Though this accelerated process does not actually occur in nature today from what we can observe empirically, is it so difficult to conceive that the God who is presented in Scripture as the Creator of all things can cause just this type of speedy growth? Certainly, our Savior Jesus was able as God on earth to quickly restore human tissue in extreme cases. Consider those He healed: a man born blind, the paralytic by the pool of Bethesda, lepers, etc. Such also were the abilities of the prophets of God, such as Elijah and Elisha. Jesus was able to make bread and fish out of a few morsels of each in the feeding of the five thousand. This miraculous event seems to have occurred as He was dividing the food and handing it to the disciples. I like the description offered by C .S. Lewis of the creation of Narnia by Aslan:

> And as he [Aslan] walked and sang the valley grew green with grass. It spread out from the Lion like a pool. It ran up the sides of the little hills like a wave. In a few minutes it was creeping up the lower slopes of the distant mountains, making that young world every moment softer . . .
>
> It was a little, spiky thing that grew out dozens of arms and covered these arms with green and grew larger at the rate of about an inch every two seconds. There were dozens of these things all round him now. When they were nearly as tall as himself he saw what they were. "Trees!" he exclaimed.[181]

We are taught from Genesis 1 that God created plants, trees, fish, fowl, creeping things, and cattle "after their kind."[182] A fuller discussion of what exactly was indicated by the term "kind" (Hebrew *mîn*: pronounced as one would pronounce "mean") is appropriate. Readily affirming the divine nature and authority of the biblical text, one would begin this investigation with the sound hermeneutical principle of looking first at "kind" within the

---

[181] C. S. Lewis, *The Magician's Nephew*, (Collier, 1970): 104–5.

[182] A good scholarly treatise focusing on the use of "kind" is that of Pete J. Williams, "What Does *min* mean?" *CENTech Journal* 11:3 (1997): 344–52.

same paragraph, then within successively larger contexts, such as the rest of the same chapter, then within the same book. The research would continue into books by the same author if any, then to other biblical books, then to other contemporaneous cognate languages in a literary context, then to later developments of the original language. In this case, understanding the use of the word *mîn* first in Genesis 1, then in the rest of Genesis, then in other Pentateuch books would the appropriate sequence. This research should be followed by looking at other occurrences in other OT books, followed by examining any cognate words to be found in the contemporaneous Semitic languages, followed by later developments in Hebrew, from Rabbinical teachings up to and including modern times. At times, some of this information may be either not readily available or simply lacking altogether. Imposing scientific taxonomies and conclusions would be the very last step in the process at determining meaning for the term under discussion. Instead of imposing science on the text, one should first let the divinely inspired and authoritative text speak for itself.

One may make several observations derived from the literary framework of the narrative of Genesis 1 before considering the specific meaning of *mîn*. There is a specific patterning in the cycles of command, fulfillment, assessment, and sequential time repeated on each of the six days. The commandment of God (expressed by the jussive of command throughout Genesis 1) that these things were to exist was indeed fulfilled, which fact is affirmed on days two, three, four, and six by the phrase "and it was so" (*way^{e}hî kēn*), which elsewhere indicates a state of completion (Judg. 6:38; 2 Kings. 15:12). When God saw that His commandment had been completed, He assessed it as "good" (*ṭôb*),[183] a word that can

[183] The comment is omitted on day two. On the sixth day, "it was good" occurs after the creation of the land animals. "It was very good" is the summary assessment of the entire creation.

mean "wholeness" or "completeness" and never means disease or death.[184] This assessment is then followed by the time sequencing involved in the phrase "and there was evening, and there was morning, the xth day." This repeated pattern, employing similar phraseology on each subsequent day, would indicate in each case that the full variety of kinds came to be in the course of a single day, and no further development or evolution would be necessary for any given created kind[185] to successfully survive in the environment that existed on subsequent days.[186]

With the preliminary presuppositions laid out as stated above, one can now begin to focus on the term at hand. On the third day of the creation week, God reveals that He created certain plants and trees after their "kind" (1:11–12). He does not tell us specifically which plants or trees that He made, but there may be three groups indicated: one simply listed as "vegetation," *deše'* (thought by some to be inedible plants), another as edible vegetation (*'ēśeb*), and the final as *'ēṣîm* (trees).[187] Each of these latter two is qualified by the designations "bearing seeds" and "yielding fruit." At the very least this could indicate their ability to produce food in the form of seeds, and, inferentially, to reproduce naturally without the cultivation of man.[188]

---

184 One notes at this point the strong contrast between life/good and death/evil in Deuteronomy 30:15.

185 Some creationist biologists employ the term *baramin*, an English word based on the Hebrew *bārā'* "to create" and *mîn* "kind." On the advice of a small group of friends, I have opted not to directly equate the two here.

186 It may be that subsequent changes to the created order that may have occurred at the fall of man in chapter 3 of Genesis and that certainly occurred as a result of the great flood of Noah (Gen. 6–8) could have brought about the ultimate extinction of certain created kinds.

187 Umberto Cassuto argued that only two categories, plants and trees, are in view as epexegetical to the general term "vegetation." Cf. Cassuto, *A Commentary on the Book of Genesis, Part 1: From Adam to Noah,* (Magnes Press, Jerusalem, 1961): 40. By epexegetical is meant here that the initial term vegetation *deše'* is broad and may be explained by the naming of the *'ēśeb* and the *'ēṣîm.*

188 Cultivable plants are mentioned in 2:5, as indicated that they were "of the field" needing both rain and human cultivation for growth. They are therefore distinct from these in Genesis 1. The viewpoint of the present author leaves open the possibility of change occurring after the fall and post–flood. It may be possible that the plants, trees, and animal types created in the first six days were different than what we observe today, but there

On day five, God creates the fish and fowl after their "kind" (1:21). In this case, all fish (referred to as the great sea creatures and the teeming creatures that teem in the waters) and all fowl ("bird of wing") that reproduce naturally seem to be in view. One notes that every kind of water creature and bird was created on day five. They did not evolve from a lower species, they were fully formed, capable of surviving in the seas or on the earth as they existed on that day, and capable of reproducing like kinds. We shall see below that the concept of *mîn* may include the ability of the fauna to develop breeds and for the flora to develop cultivars.

Day six also employs the term *mîn*. On that day, God makes the land animals "according to their kind" (1:24). These include cattle (*bᵉhēmâ*), which may include sheep, goats, etc., creeping things (*remeś*), which may refer to insects and arachnids at least, and the "life of the earth" (every other type of animal based on dry land). These animals as they were created on day six would have had the ability to survive on the earth as it existed on that day, and would have had the ability to reproduce offspring within their own "created kind." One may also suggest that God made man on the same day after *His* own kind, since He made man as His representative (image) to the rest of creation (expressed by the *bêt essentiae* on the word *ṣelem* as well as in the term "according to His likeness" in 1:26. See discussion in the next chapter). We are therefore like God to a degree, and represent Him to the remainder of the creation, but different from Him significantly due to our finiteness.

---

is still no evidence of any species evolving into new species anywhere in the Genesis record. Yet, despite changes beginning to occur with the event of the fall (with the advent of disease and death) and continuing to occur in the post–flood world (assuming an environment significantly changed), it is still possible that the "created kinds" we observe today are similar to the earlier varieties. In other words, a horse during the creation week would be similar to a horse today, and identifiable as a horse. One would have called it neither a woodchuck nor an eagle!

One encounters the term "kind" again in the flood narrative from Genesis 6–9. In Genesis 6:20, God instructs Noah to take with him on the ark birds, animals, and creeping things, each "after its kind." This is followed in 7:14 by the actual obedience to the command wherein the beasts, cattle, creeping things and birds come on the ark, all described with the phrase "after its kind." The occurrence of that phrase after the mention of the birds may be explained by the following phrase in Hebrew, literally "every bird, every wing." Some translators have understood this as "all sorts of birds" which stands in apposition to "kind." If this is the correct reading, then "kind" could involve here the idea of differing breeds. Indeed, this seems to be the understanding in the next nearest passage (in Leviticus) that employs *mîn*.

In the legal passages describing kosher dietary laws, the term *mîn* comes up again a number of times. Leviticus 11:14–19 refer to birds of prey that are not to be eaten by those who live under the Mosaic covenant. Parallels with minor differences are found in listing of kosher foods in Deuteronomy 14:12–19. As an example for the purpose of comparison, whereas flying things are generalized in Genesis 1 and major groups of flying things may be understood in Genesis 7, individual species may be involved in Leviticus 11 and Deuteronomy 14. This is evidenced by the differences in the Hebrew nouns used in the dietary lists, many of which are *hapax legomena* (found only once in Scripture), and thus making any exact designation difficult to determine for the twenty types of flying creatures involved in Leviticus 11.[189]

It seems at this point that *mîn* might refer to subcategories of the term to which it refers. In other words, in Genesis 1 *mîn* might refer to subcategories of flying things, and

[189] Twenty–one types in Deuteronomy 14 which adds a red kite to the list.

Genesis 6–7 *mîn* might refer to the subcategories of those subcategories. In Leviticus 11 and Deuteronomy 14, the terms for the birds (and in Lev. 11 the creeping things) are more refined, more specific. Therefore the presence of *mîn* in those passages may often indicate subspecies or breeds. This seems to be the case as well in the final biblical occurrence of *mîn*, which deals with kinds of fish in Ezekiel 47:10.

A final point that the reader may find useful is the fact that in Rabbinical Hebrew, the term *mîn* was used to describe a Jewish convert to Christ, which we would call a Messianic Jew. These are not understood to be as radically different from the Jews as are the *gôyîm*, the Gentiles. The *mînîm* are rather those like the Jews, still Jewish, but different from them in that they believe that Jesus of Nazareth is their Jewish Messiah.

The fourth day (Gen. 1:10–14) is important as it is another day of the creative activity of God. On this day, the Scriptures tell us that He created the sun, moon, and stars. To be sure, the normal term for sun (*šemeš*) is not used, nor is that of moon (*yarēaḥ*), ostensibly due to the fact that these orbs were worshiped as gods by pagan nations (the names of later biblical cities Beth–Shemesh and Jericho testify to this practice).[190] Instead, the Bible refers to these orbs as lights,[191] modified by the adjectives "greater" and "lesser" or "larger" and "smaller" depending on the translation.

We are also told in verse 16 that God also made the stars on the fourth day. I have personally heard a well–known young earth astronomer twice present his understanding that the stars possibly predate Genesis 1. Pulling him aside privately after his first presentation, I challenged him gently just at this point for the following reason. In Hebrew narrative, a

---

[190] These same lights are named specifically as "sun" and "moon" in the poetical allusion to the creation event in Psalm 136:7–9.

[191] The designation of the "lesser light" as referring to the moon is perhaps phenomological language, much in the sense of saying "the sun rises." No one doubts that the full moon provides significant light to the earth, albeit reflective light.

definite direct object of a verb is easily identified with the particle *'ēt*. This particle may be immediately before the direct object in the text or actually affixed to it with a *maqqeph* (like a hyphen).[192] A single verb may govern several direct objects, and each will then be marked by its own separate *'ēt* particle. Such is the case in 1:16, where the verb *wayyaʿaś* ("so He made") governs "the two great lights," "the greater light," "the lesser light," and "the stars," and each of these direct objects has its own separate direct object marker *'ēt*. This indicates that they were all created in response to God's command, and most likely at the same time, as they are followed in verse nineteen with the temporal summary "and there was evening and there was morning, *the* fourth day." This understanding is supported as well by Exodus 20:11: "For six days the Lord made the heavens and the earth and the sea, and all that are **in them**."[193]

On the fifth day (Gen. 1:20–23), God created aquatic life which would become very numerous to the point of "teeming" or "swarming" and would with His blessing "fill the waters of the seas" (1:23). Cassuto has said: "The fecundity of the fish, which is so great as to have become proverbial, is indicative of the special blessing that was bestowed on them at the time of their creation."[194] These creatures are described on day five not as "fish" (*dāg*), but as "the great sea monsters" as well as "every living creature that moves, with which the waters swarmed after their kind" (NASV). However, the latter description must have included "fish," as they are specifically named by the next day (1:26). The term translated by

---

[192] The Hebrew student will note a reduction in the vowel from a *ṣērē* to a *seghol* when this particle is affixed to the direct object by means of the *maqqeph*. In Genesis 1:16 the first three occurrences are thus reduced in the presence of the *maqqeph*, the fourth is not.

[193] I have emboldened the phrase "in them" because the Hebrew preposition is suffixed with a third masculine plural morpheme, the antecedent to which includes "the heavens and the earth and the sea," the first of which would have included the luminaries and the stars.

[194] Cassuto, *Genesis*, 51.

the NASV as "sea monsters" and by the KJV as "whales" is the Hebrew noun *tannînim*,[195] a masculine plural form. Cassuto rightly notes that "only the general categories of plants and animals are mentioned, but not the separate species, save the sea monsters. This exception has not been made, we may be sure, without a specific motive."[196] This motive, of course, seems to be a specific polemic offered against the mythologies of other nations, particularly those of the Akkadians, Babylonians, and Canaanites, all of which mythologies have great sea monsters rising up in rebellion against the gods who had to subdue them in order to create the heavens and the earth. But it is just as likely that the text of Genesis 1 and/or the oral recitation of the text predated the mythologies of those nations. In other words, the mythologies may have been derived from the story of Genesis 1 rather than Genesis 1 being written later as a polemic against the mythologies of those nations. Either priority is possible, but the authoritative God-given Scripture must be held preeminently as recording the actual events.

For the sake of argument, one may say for a moment that the actual case is that Genesis 1 served as a polemic against the cosmologies of other nations. For this reason, God points out that the *tannînim* were totally under His control from the beginning, that they were created in the natural order of things, and that they are to join the created order in offering praise to YHWH (cf. Ps. 147:7).

What then were these *tannînim*? The excellent lexicon by Brown, Driver, and Briggs suggests that the root *tannîn* is an Aramaic loan word and has a later development into the

[195] Hebrew students, observing the text in BHS, should notice that the masculine plural ending is written defectively, i.e., without the *mater lectionis yôd.*
[196] Cassuto, 49.

fish named *thynnos* in Greek.[197] BDB offers the gloss of "serpent, dragon, sea–monster"[198] for *tannîn* but one notes that the word is different from the serpent of Genesis 3:1 (*naḥaš*), and different as well from the "great fish" (*dāg gādôl*) of Jonah; and therefore should not be equated in translations that may not otherwise distinguish between them.

The word *tannîn* is found nowhere else in Genesis, but occurs elsewhere in the MT. By far, the KJV translates most of those occurrences as "dragons" or "whales" (see chart). The *tannînim*[199] are most frequently associated with the sea (Ezek. 29:3, 32:2; Job 7:12; Pss. 74:13; 148:7; Isa. 27:1 (//Leviathan), 51:9 (//Rahab); Lam. 4:3; Jer. 51:34) but also are at times associated with land and probably mean "serpents" (Exod. 7:9, 10, 12; Neh. 2:13; Deut. 32:33; Ps. 91:13 where both // "cobras"). The various modern translations will translate it as whale, jackal, serpent, dragon, snake, and sea monster.

[197] BDB, 1072. Neither of these facts necessitate a later date for Genesis 1 due to the presence of what BDB calls an Aramaic loan word. A plausible response could be that since the earlier Hebrew scripts known to Moses, David, and the kings were converted to Aramaic square script in the time of Ezra, some updating of original archaic terms may have been made at that time.

[198] BDB, 1072.

[199] The plural is consistently written defectively, that is, without the expected *mater yôd*.

Nine: The Sixth Day Genesis 1:24–31

In keeping with the first five days of creation, the sixth day[200] begins with God issuing yet another jussive of command in order to bring land-based animals, as well as man, into existence. In each of the first five commands, division takes place in the process. Day one brings light from the darkness. Day two brings a separation of the waters to produce the heavens. On day three, the seas are separated by dry land, on which the vegetation sprouts. In day four the great lights are created to make a clear division between day and night. One may argue that on day five, God separated the fish from the water and the birds from the sky.[201]

---

[200] There is an anomaly on the sixth day with the Hebrew syntax. Whereas the second through fifth days are all anarthrous (without the article), the construction of the sixth day reveals an ordinal with an article: *yôm haššiššî*. This construction provides a minor difficulty in the hypothesis developed elsewhere in this book, but is easily explained. First of all, the presence of the article on the ordinal "sixth" here does not happen on the earlier examples. This might seem to indicate a construct relationship similar to the use of *yôm* in construct with other nouns. Thus at first glance, it alone out of all the occurrences of *yôm* with an ordinal in Genesis 1 seems to support the hypothesis of Hugh Ross that such constructions elsewhere in the Old Testament allow for a nonliteral use of *yôm* (i.e., not as a twenty-four-hour day) in Genesis 1. However, this syntax of a noun bound to an ordinal in a construct relationship is very scarce elsewhere in the MT. All the examples Ross points to are examples of nouns in construct with other nouns, not a noun in construct with an ordinal, as might or might not be the case here. The syntax of a noun in construct with another noun does not exist in Genesis 1:1–2:3 with *yôm*. Too this phrase certainly does not allow for an aspect of an indefinite period of time. In fact, the opposite is true. It is literally "day the sixth." So what does this mean? Bound relationships express genitive case aspects. For instance, "the love of Christ constrains me" (2 Cor. 5:14) can be either "Christ's love" or "love for Christ." The proper interpretation is contextually determined. So it is here. In the case of 1:30, if it is a noun in construct with an ordinal number, the best genitive classification is an appositional genitive "the day which is the sixth day" (cf. Ronald J. Williams, *Hebrew Syntax, An Outline*, 2nd ed., U. of Toronto, 1976, 21). Thus, though one might take note of the special construction's significance of the sixth day as developed further in chapter 2 (creation of man, planting of garden, creation of woman, etc.), the syntax is absolutely consistent with the pattern of the second to fifth days, including the further apposition with the repeated "and there was evening and there was morning."

[201] Whether the fish and/or the birds were created from physical materials of their elements *in situ* or created separately and placed therein is not stated in the text.

Day six is no different, since it is from the ground that the Lord God creates both beast and man.

As it has been a problem for some that the earth was fully vegetated within a day's time, so others also find incredible the description of the creation of land-based animals within a similar time frame. Yet, this is just what the text indicates. God issued His creative decree, "Let the earth bring forth living creatures after their kind" (NASV). Following the decree, the expected statement of completion is given "and it was so." Here again, our analogy of time–lapse photography is illustrated in Aslan's creation of the animals:

> Can you imagine a stretch of grassy land bubbling like water in a pot? For that is really the best description of what was happening. In all directions it was swelling into humps. There were of very different sizes, some no bigger than mole–hills, some as big as wheel–barrows, two the size of cottages. And the humps moved and swelled till they burst, and the crumbled earth poured out of them, and from each hump there came out an animal.[202]

This of course is an imaginative passage from fiction, but it could offer a plausible understanding of the initial events of day six, which the text affirms occurred all within a twenty-four-hour period as we understand it.[203] If so, the Scripture, by portraying a miracle in minimal time, stands in sharp contrast not only with slower processes of growth and development, which are observable today, but also with Darwinism, the conclusions of which are derived from those same contemporary observations.

One must notice again the use of the phrase "after its kind." As discussed above on day three with the plant life and on day five with the fish and fowl, the animals to be based on land were created on the sixth day, each after their kind. These included the general

---

[202] C. S. Lewis, 113.

[203] James Barr, noted Old Testament scholar who taught at Oxford and later at Vanderbilt, once wrote: "So far as I know, there is no professor of Hebrew or Old Testament at any world–class university who does not believe that the writer(s) of Genesis1–11 intended to convey to their readers the ideas that (a) creation took place in a series of six days which were the same as the days of twenty-four-hours we now experience. . . ." (James Barr, Letter to David C.C. Watson, 1984: Quoted in *CENTech Journal*, 1995).

groupings of cattle, creeping things, and animal life of the earth.[204] This verse, understood normally within the grammatico–historical interpretive parameters with a verbal, plenary view of inerrant inspiration, clearly cannot be harmonized with Darwinistic evolution, as at least three separate groups (besides man) were created on the same twenty-four-hour day. So instead of a single evolutionary tree, the Bible seems to suggest that there is actually a forest of created kinds.

The Special Creation of Man

It is probably safe to say that one of the most quoted parts of Scripture is that "man is created in the image of God." It is perhaps also one of the most misunderstood passages in the Hebrew Bible. This is due in part to the fact there is confusion in many quarters over just what the English translations entail. In other words, does the phrase indicate corporeality? Are we intended to "look" like God? Do we "bear" the image of God? If this is the case, is this all it means? Does God therefore exist corporeally? Certainly God is said in Scripture to have a face, eyes, nose, mouth, arm, hand, etc., but these terms are normally understood to be anthropomorphisms, i.e., figures of speech attributing to God the physical attributes of humans. Too, He is clearly called "spirit" (John 4:24) and "light" (I John 1:5). On the other hand, He did appear at times in the Old Testament as the "angel of YHWH" thought by Christians to be the pre–incarnate Christ appearing as a man. It is my contention that a careful study of the words involved in 1:26 and the syntax employed there will yield a clearer and hopefully more plausible understanding of what God intended us to know about who we are and what our role should be in the created order.

The phrase in the MT at 1:26–27 has been translated traditionally as:

---

[204] The initial phrase "living creatures after their kind" may be a topic statement developed by the three groups that follow.

> Let us make man in our image according to our likeness (*b**ṣalmēnû kidmûtēnû*); and let them rule (*w**yirdû*) over the fish of the sea and over the birds of the sky and over the cattle and over all the earth, and over all the creeping things that creep upon the earth. So God created man in his image; in the image of God He created him, male and female He created them.

The key terms that need to be considered here lexicographically are the Hebrew nouns *ṣelem*, *d*^{e}*mût*, and the verb *rādâ*.

The term "image" translated in most versions is the Hebrew word *ṣelem*, normally associated with idols in the Old Testament outside of Genesis. For instance, in Numbers 33:52 God tells Moses to instruct the Israelites to destroy all the molten idols of the Canaanites. In 2 Kings 11:18, the term describes the destruction of images depicting Baal. In Amos 5:26, the word is used to depict the idols of specific pagan deities carried by the Israelites into the wilderness following the exodus. The same word in Aramaic is used in Daniel 2 (vv. 31, 32, 34, 35) and Daniel 3 (vv. 1, 2, 3 {2x}, 5, 7, 10, 12, 14, 15, 18, 19) repeatedly to refer first to the image Nebuchadnezzar sees in his dream and then to the actual image he erected on the plain of Dura in Babylon to be worshiped by all. Other usages include 1 Sam. 6:5, 11 where the Philistines produced images of mice and tumors made from gold to send with the ark of the covenant back to Beth–Shemesh. Images that represent humans or body parts may be indicated with the use of the word *ṣelem* in Ezekiel 16:17 and 23:14.

Reflecting on the way the term *ṣelem* is used in other parts of Scripture outside of Genesis seems to indicate a conception of a representation of some sort depicting one's understanding of the person or false gods being considered. I prefer the gloss of "representative" for the word (see the discussion below). It is at first glance interesting that God would choose this word *ṣelem* for us as His creatures, especially in view of the fact that the word normally indicates idols. But upon reflection, one comes to see the brilliance of this word choice in that the idols represent dead gods who cannot think, act, move, hear, or see. We on the other hand are designed to represent the living God; hence, we live as He lives.

The second noun to be considered in our study is *d*^{e}*mût*, a word normally understood as "likeness," as it is derived from the verbal root *dāmâ*, which means to "be like, resemble."[205] Since the root idea includes the idea of a comparison, the figure of speech called simile may be inherently in view. Whenever simile comes into play, it is necessary to try to find the point of comparison that is intended by the author. Thus it is translated "likeness" throughout the vision of Ezekiel chapter 1 to describe indescribable things in the best way possible. In Daniel 10:16 the term is used to describe what is ostensibly the visible manifestation of an angelic being ("as the likeness of the sons of men"). Daniel's point is that the being attending him looked like a man in physical appearance. Isaiah uses both the verb and the noun when he asks in 40:18: "To whom will you compare God, and what likeness would you arrange for Him?" Isaiah's point is that God is incomparable. This fact makes John 1:18 very exciting: Jesus is the one who has fully interpreted God to us![206] It seems, therefore, that a good understanding for *demût* in Genesis 1:26 would be simply a comparison in some sense. Prefixed with the inseparable preposition *k*, normally meaning "according to," the sense seems to be that God was planning to make men in some way reflecting who He is in His character and being, rather than simply "looking" like Him in some physical, corporeal way.

---

[205] BDB, 197.

[206] The Greek word here is actually *exegēomai*, the word from which we derive our verb to exegete, meaning to interpret from the original language. An exegesis then is an interpretation derived from the text, rather than reading into it, which is eisegesis.

The third term to consider is the verb *rādâ*, which is normally understood as to "have dominion, rule."[207] It is a word that is used in passages to describe the *rule* that Messiah will ultimately have. Psalm 110:2 offers the command of the Lord that His chosen king *rule* in the midst of His enemies. A similar idea occurs in the prophecy of Balaam in Numbers 24:19: "and he will *rule* from Jacob." In 1 Kings 4:24, Solomon is said to have *ruled* over all lands west of the Euphrates during the Golden Age of Israel. The idea then of the verb *rādâ* used here in 1:26 seems therefore to indicate a rulership appropriate for great kings.

One must also consider the use of the *bêt* preposition prefixed to the noun *ṣelem* in 1:26. While the phrase *b^eṣalmēnû* has traditionally been translated "in our image" it is just as easily translated "as our image." This would understand the preposition *bêt* syntactically as a *bêt essentiae*, or a *bêt* of essence.[208] This means that the preposition holds the meaning "serving as," and may be illustrated by its use in Exodus 6:3: "and I appeared to Abraham, to Isaac, and to Jacob ***as*** God almighty" and Psalm 54:6: "The Lord is ***as*** those who support my soul."

With this study in hand, one may then translate the passage thusly: "Then God said, 'Let us make man as our representative, like us, and let him have dominion. . . .'" Translating the passage in this way alleviates any problem with the idea of man "looking" like God, but in no way impinges on the concept that we share certain characteristics of the Creator.[209] We

---

[207] BDB, 921.

[208] That a *bêt* can serve in this way is affirmed in the excellent grammar/syntax of Waltke and O'Connor, 198; and specifically affirmed in this passage by Allen Ross, *Creation and Blessing*, 112.

[209] A peripheral benefit of understanding image instead as "representative" may be seen in the interpretation of two psalms. In Psalm 39:5, the NASV renders the passage: "Surely every man walks about as a phantom, surely they make an uproar for nothing" where *b^eṣelem* is translated as "as a phantom." Were this passage to be rendered "Indeed man walks about as a representative (of God), yet surely they make an uproar for nothing" would make good antithetic parallelism in view of the final synthetic idea in the third clause: "He amasses *riches* and does not know who will gather them" (NASV). In Psalm 73:20, the NASV's rendition is: "Like a dream when one awakes, O Lord, when aroused, You will despise their form." In the immediate context, the

are like God in that He shares His communicable attributes with man in order that we might appear as godly king-like rulers to the rest of creation.

This understanding has several implications. First, it takes both genders, male and female, to represent God fully. He could have done it with only one but chose two instead. Certain attributes of God are best displayed by men; other attributes of God are best displayed by women. This means that women and men are equal before God, and have equal responsibility before God to properly govern the creation in the unique ways that God has given to them.

Second, we have a responsibility to care for the creation. This passage indicates that our responsibility to have dominion runs from fish to birds to land animals to insect life, but it also includes the phrase "over all the earth." That it extends to flora as well could be a strong implication from the responsibility God gave Adam in the garden of Eden to "watch and keep it" (2:15). That being said, as the very representatives of God to the created order, we are tasked with a commitment to the environment in general, to plant and animal life specifically, and certainly to one another as fellow representatives of God.

Our ability to fulfill our responsibility to represent God well was certainly diminished by the fall, which explains why mankind exploits both the environment and each other with reckless abandon. The fall explains why historically men generally have dominated women, and why women have desired to dominate men (cf. Gen. 3:16). The fall explains why there is strife and warfare (cf. Gen. 4), why there is sickness and death (Gen. 2:17; 3:16), and this latter fact provides a plausible possibility for anomalies such as birth defects. Yet the responsibility remains ours as human beings to represent God well. Because of the fall, it is

---

psalmist is being reminded of the ultimate destruction of the wicked. Were one to translate instead: "Like a dream when one awakes, O Lord, when aroused, You will despise their representation." In other words, sinful man does not accomplish what God intended for him when He bestowed on him the title of "representative."

most likely that the only way individuals can regain balance and authority to fully accomplish our responsibilities as humans is to join in relationship to the one person God provided to redeem us. This of course is Jesus, who is the sin–bearer, the perfect "image" (representative) of the invisible God (Col. 1:15). He is the one who "exegeted" or interpreted God (John 1:18) in order to give us a visible physical example to follow.

It seems then that God intended mankind as His representative (*ṣelem*) and as reflecting who He is in His character as being like Him (*d*ᵉ*mût*) in order to have dominion (*rādâ*) as godly rulers over the created order.

The remainder of chapter 1 of the creation narrative includes the blessing that God gave the man and the woman as well as God's final assessment of the results of the creative process. This blessing involves the first use of the term *bārak* (1:27), which word becomes extremely important not only with reference to the person of God but also in reference to His relationship with His people Israel (cf. Deut. 28). In His blessing of the original man and the woman, God instructs them to be fruitful, multiply, and fill the earth (1:28a). We certainly have done a good job of obeying that instruction! Too, mankind is to fulfill their purpose as God's living representatives over the creation, ruling over it (1:28b; cf. 1:26 above). God grants first to mankind, then to the animal kingdom, permission to eat the plants and trees He has provided for their sustenance (1:29–30). In His assessment of the final state of the heavens and earth after six days of His creative activity, God finds all to be "very good" (1:31). Though discussed elsewhere in the present work, it should be noted here that the term *ṭôb* is associated with life and well–being in the rest of the Old Testament. God assesses it as "very good," which assessment seems to be at least comparative, and at most superlative. The earth was without sin, without disease, and without death. All was harmonious in nature, and needed no further evolutionary development to function properly. God could safely cease His creative activity, which He will do on the seventh day.

Ten: The Insights of Genesis 2

There is an unfortunate chapter break after 1:31. Genesis 2:1–3 really belongs to the creation pericope started in 1:1 for three reasons. First, it continues the past tense narrative sequencing started with the perfect tense verb of 1:2 and followed throughout chapter 1 by means of the series of preterite verbs with *waw* consecutive. Second, it completes the creation week by revealing the information relative to the seventh day, the day of God's rest. Third, Genesis 2:1 introduces the final section of the creation pericope by offering an *inclusio,* which ties 2:1–3 in with 1:1ff. This is seen in the repetition of the phrase "heavens and earth."

The patterning of the seventh day, however, is different from the other six in many ways. First of all, there is no creative activity by God at all recorded on this day. Instead, God rested (*wayiššbōt*) from His work, which He had finished (*waykal*). More will be said about these terms below. Second, the seventh day alone has *yôm* with the article, which may indicate a difference in quality even though it says nothing about duration.[210] Third, there are no commands by God but only a blessing and a setting apart. Fourth, there is no repetition of the phrase "and there was evening and there was morning." Fifth, there was no assessment of completion, expressed earlier by *wayᵉhî kēn*. Sixth, there was no assessment of "goodness."

Since the verb introducing chapter 2 is a preterite with waw consecutive, continuing the narrative account, and since it states that the heavens and the earth and all their hosts

[210] In other words, *yôm* still means a twenty-four-hour day. That fact is not affected by the presence of an article.

were then finished, and since this expression occurs immediately following the assessment and naming of the sixth day, it follows that the use of the same verb with God as subject in 2:2 should be understood as a past perfect: "God had finished." Therefore, NASV rightly captures the sense of the preposition *bêt* "*by* the seventh day." Notice the nuanced change with the same preposition in the next phrase, which first introduces the concept of "rest."

We are told in 2:2 that God rested on the seventh day from all His labor, which He had done. Unfortunately, this rendering at least hints at the possibility that the work of creation had left God in need of respite. Nothing could be further from the truth. Indeed, we should probably understand the verb *wayiššbōt* differently than "and He rested." The form in the text offers the root *šābat*, from which the nominal form *šabbat* has been loaned to us as "Sabbath." Though we know this as a day of rest, the emphasis of the verb itself in Scripture seems to be rather that it is a cessation of previous activities. Certainly this seems to be the idea of *šābat* in Joshua 5:12, when the manna offered in the wilderness *stopped* coming once the Israelites had feasted on the abundance of the Promised Land. The enemies of Judah plotted to *stop* the work on the walls of Jerusalem in Nehemiah 4:11 (MT 4:5). God promises that the postdiluvian seasons would not *cease* as long as the earth continued (Gen. 8:22). God causes all wars to *cease* (Ps. 46:9 [10]). In the present context, God had finished His work by the seventh day, so He did not create on that day. It is as simple as that.

Some seek to understand the term *yôm* on the seventh day as being somewhat timeless and thus can be used in a timeless sense on days one through six. For the most part, those who seek this understanding appeal to the fact that the phrase "and there was morning and there was evening" does not appear on the seventh day. They also appeal to the teaching of a remaining Sabbath rest for the people of God as discussed in the New Testament book of

Hebrews (4:1–11). Holding the first point for the next paragraph, the Hebrews passage uses Genesis 2:1–3 only as a supporting illustration of an ultimate rest for God's people based on God ceasing His creative activity on the seventh day. It does not affect the normal meaning of *yôm* already established on days 1–6, and thus seems inconclusive in the discussion.

It is because the seventh day is the day that God stopped His creative activity that there is no need to include the phrase concerning the evening and the morning. His stoppage of creative work only (He still providentially manages the creation) was punctiliar in aspect. Since there was to be no continuance of creative activity, since He stopped *from* His work (*mikkol–m^{e}la'ktô*), there was no need for the phrase that indicated not only time sequencing but also continuance. Thus, no "and there was evening and there was morning" was necessary. He stopped on the seventh day, He blessed it, and He set it apart (sanctified it). No more creative activity took place on that day that resembled the first six days. In fact, the duration of time indicated by the term "day" is sufficiently defined on the first six days that no further qualification is needed on the seventh day, one of cessation from work. The seventh day was therefore unique in the creation week and as such was uniquely described.

The Detailed Creation of Man and Woman

As Genesis 2:3 concludes the Bible's cosmology, the general account of original creation, 2:4 introduces the specifics of the occurrences on day six. Specifically, the creation of man and woman is in view. Much has been said in the discourses through the ages about the seeming inconsistencies between the two accounts. Some have seen these alleged differences as demanding differing authorship, differing provenances, and differing traditions. However, when seen as typical narrative sequencing following introductory clauses, the action that begins in 2:7 with the preterite verb with *wāw* consecutive immediately following a setting offered in 2:5–6 (as 1:3 follows 1:2) ties the two sections together nicely.

Regarding the alleged differences, Cassuto has given the scholarly world much clarification on the issues involved. One of the complaints of some has been that chapter 1 names six days of creation, whereas 2:4 names only one: "in the day." As mentioned earlier, and though St. Augustine thereby understood a single day of creation, "in the day" with an infinitive construct (as here) simply and idiomatically exists as a time indicator and may safely be translated as "when."[211]

Still others who seek to find inconsistencies with the two chapters make much of the fact that chapter 1 contains only the name *ʾĕlōhîm* for God, whereas chapter two introduces *yhwh* in the combined form *yhwh ʾĕlōhîm*. Umberto Cassuto powerfully addresses this issue when he writes:

> For these reasons the name *YHWH* was required in this section, and this is the name that we actually find. Its association, however, with the appellation *'Elōhīm*, which is restricted to this one section of the entire book, is easily explained by Scripture's desire to teach us that *YHWH*, which occurs here for the first time, is to be wholly identified with *'Elōhīm* mentioned in the preceding section; in other words, that the God of the moral world is none other than the God of the material world, that the God of Israel is in fact the God of the entire universe, and that the names *YHWH* and *'Elōhīm* merely indicate two different facets of His activity or two different ways in which He reveals Himself to mankind.[212]

Still another seeming inconsistency is that chapter 1 starts with water then dry land, and chapter two seems to start with dry land with no mention of seas. Cassuto points out that there is no reason to mention the oceans, as chapter two is not a cosmogony, as is chapter 1, but rather a detailed description of the events of day six. He writes:

---

[211] Cf. Cassuto, *Commentary on Genesis I*, 89.
[212] Ibid., 88. The reader of this book would do well to thoroughly investigate Cassuto's discussion on this issue.

> When we read the Torah as we have it, as a continuous narrative, we find no discrepancy between the earlier statement that at first the world was a mass of water, and what we are told about the dry land at the beginning of the present section. Relying on the account of the first stages of creation given above, our section does not recapitulate the story; it depicts simply the position as it was at the *closing phase* of creation when man alone was wanting.[213]

In other words, 2:4ff pick up on day six just before Man was specially created by God and just before Woman was artistically built by God for Man.

The section in chapter two offering the specifics of the creation of man and woman is introduced by the phrase "These are the generations of the heavens and the earth." This phrase is based on the Hebrew word for generations, *tôl^{e}dôt*, which word serves as a structural indicator in the book of Genesis. Since the plural noun *tôl^{e}dôt* is formed from the root *yālad*, which means "to beget" in the masculine gender and "to bear" in the feminine, many scholars like to see a nuance of production in the term. In other words, *tôl^{e}dôt* could refer here to that which the heavens and earth produced, much in the same way that the further uses of *tôl^{e}dôt* involve the offspring of the patriarchs of the book of Genesis (Adam in 5:1, Noah in 6:9, the sons of Noah in 10:1, Isaac in 25:19, Jacob in 37:2, etc.). In the case of 2:4, that which the earth brought forth by the hand of God was Adam from the dust and Eve taken from Adam.

As prelude to the special creation of Man in 2:7, the narrator sets the stage for the reader in 2:5–6, as each of these verses begin with a waw disjunctive ("Now...") . We are told in 2:5 that there was neither yet sprout[214] nor cultivable plant on the earth due to the fact that God had not yet brought rain on the earth[215] nor was there man to cultivate the plants.

---

[213] Cassuto, *Genesis*, 90.

[214] The Hebrew term *śîaḥ* is interpreted by Cassuto to equal "thorns and thistles" (*Genesis*, pp. 101–2).

[215] Rain is not mentioned again until Genesis 6. Because of this many see the antediluvian world as watered by the system mentioned in 2:6 until the time of the flood. However, it is an argument from silence to base any theory on the existence of rain before the flood, or the commencement of rain only at the flood.

This does not negate the words of chapter 1 as it discussed the vegetation of day three, as the vocabulary in chapter 2 qualifies the vegetation as being "of the field" looking forward to Adam's punishment in chapter 3 mandating that he work the land from which he came in order to eat bread. In 1:11–12, the trees and vegetation were self–propagating, having seeds within them. In gardening terms, these were the annuals, having no need of man's cultivation to survive and propagate.

Genesis 2:6 offers yet another bit of information about the pre–Adam, pre–fall world. It was not watered by rain, but rather by a "mist" that used to go up from the earth and give drink to the soil. Since the term *'ēd* exists only in this verse and in Job 36:27, the precise meaning is difficult to determine. Several suggested glosses include "mist," "vapor," "springs," and "streams."

It was into this recently created environment that God began to form His pinnacle of creation: mankind. The text narrates to us that He began with man, which he took from the ground, then completed His work with woman whom He took from the man. The text does not state that the man was at first created as male and female combined, from which God took the feminine parts to create woman. It is not stated in those terms. Instead, whatever gender characteristics man had prior to woman are not stated. However, that being said, the text offers wording that indicates maleness for Adam and femaleness for the Woman. This is seen in the consistency of the pronominal suffixes used throughout the passage for both individuals, as well as the appropriate verbal forms for each gender.

God "formed" the man. The verb employed here is *yāṣar*. It is the same verb used of the potter who fashions clay into a useable vessel in Jeremiah 18:2, and involves both purpose and design. Isaiah 44:2 and 49:5 both speak of the involvement of God in the formation of the fetus in the womb. Thus God had both purpose and design as He intimately formed man. The material God used to make man was taken from the earth He had recently made. It was dust (*'āp̱ar*). The Psalmist reminds us that God is mindful that we are but dust (Ps. 103:14). Never associated with any value in Scripture, dust is often instead associated with death (Gen. 3:19; Ps. 22:15; Dan. 12:2). Though taken from the earth, the form God fashioned from the dust was inanimate; lifeless until God gave it life. We are told by the narrator that God breathed into man's nostrils the breath of life. Only then did man become a living being.

The term "breath of life" in Hebrew is *nišmat ḥayyîm*. The first term *nišmat* is the construct form of the noun *nᵉšāmâ*, which is worthy of further note. In chapter 1, God purposes to create man in His image (representation) and likeness. To achieve this, man must have another distinction, one that sets him apart from the rest of the animal kingdom. He must have the *nᵉšāmâ* of life. It is this *nᵉšāmâ* that gives man understanding (Job 32:8) and enables his conscience (Proverbs 20:27). It is never used of any living being other than humanity.[216] We are therefore uniquely distinguished from the animal kingdom as the representatives of God, possessing His special breath that both animates us and enables us to function in dominion over His creation. That was our role, our responsibility, and our ability before the fall. It remained our role and responsibility after the fall, but the sinfulness of man keeps him from carrying out that role in the manner that God intended.

The First Home of Adam: The Garden of God

When God had finished forming the man and given him the breath of life, the man then and only then became a living soul. God then constructed a garden into which to place

216 Cf. T.C. Mitchell, "The Old Testament Usage of Nešāma," *Vetus Testamentum* 11 (1961): 177–87.

the man, giving Adam the position of caretaker. The Lord God first planted the garden (it was in Eden, to the east), then placed man in it (2:8).[217] In 2:9, the narrator tells us that God had caused trees desirable both for their appearance and for their fruit to sprout from the soil. Among them in the garden of Eden were to be found the Tree of Life as well as the Tree of Knowledge of Good and Evil (2:9).

After this placing of man into the Garden, the narrator digresses once again to explain the watering system that existed at that time, both for the garden, and for the entire region (2:10–14). The story of the man continues in 2:15, where God causes man to dwell in the garden of Eden and gives him the responsibility both to "work it and keep it." Because of the significance of the two terms *'ābad* (work) and *šāmar* (keep) in the remainder of the Pentateuch, where they are normally referring to tabernacle ministries of "serving" and "observing (the law)," some have desired to see evidence of later editing of the text of Genesis or perhaps even evidence of the editing in of later documents, *a la* the Documentary hypothesis (discussed earlier). It may just as easily be argued that the two terms were used in Genesis 2 as examples of service to God later developed in a theological sense for service in the tabernacle (and later still in the temple). Either way, one is reminded that work is a concept of service to God developed before the fall of man. Judgment at the fall resulted in a struggle for those who labor.

When God commanded (root *ṣāwâ*, from which the crucial theological noun *miṣwâ*, "commandment" is built) Adam in 2:16 not to eat from the one tree, the Tree of the Knowledge of Good and Evil, He was also authorizing the freedom for Adam to consume the fruit from any and all of the other fruit-bearing trees in the garden. All the other trees

[217] The text is unclear whether this garden was created ahead of time on day three, or if God newly "planted" it on day six. The verbs can be either simple past or past perfects.

promote life and good. Only by eating of this tree is death a possibility. The promise of death is expressed strongly by use of the intensifying absolute infinitive *môt* placed before the verb *tāmût*, and may be translated either as "you shall certainly die," or even as "dying, you will die." The latter rendition allows for an understanding that the process of physical death will begin at the moment of disobedience and would then be a certainty. Thus this command becomes a foreshadowing for the events of chapter 3, yet the foreshadowing is not complete until the woman has been taken from Adam's side.

In 2:18–20, Adam is instructed by God to name all of the animals of the garden. This is done ostensibly because there was not as yet a helper (*'ezer*)[218] suitable for Adam (*k^{e}negdô*, one corresponding to him, i.e., a female to complement his maleness, as was evident in the rest of the animals God brought to him to name). God assessed this situation as not good, so He fixed it by making a very special woman for Adam. When Adam had named the animals brought to him, which shows his dominion over them even as it does for us today when we name our own children (but meant so much more in a pre–fall world I think), the narrator assesses that there was found no such helper for him in the garden.

As God performed the first surgery mentioned in the Scripture, He caused Adam to fall into a deep sleep and removed part of his side (the Hebrew word suggests more tissue involvement than just a rib bone) and closed up the incision. With this tissue, God built a woman (2:22). God had formed Adam as a potter molds clay, but God builds (*bānâ*) the woman as a contractor designs and builds a beautiful home.

[218] The noun "helper" is also used of God being our helper in the Psalms, so no one should conceive of this role as woman being subservient to the male. Nor on the other hand may one suggest that this means that the female should be regarded as superior to the male. Equality is initially in view, as it takes both male and female humans to properly represent the attributes of God to His creation.

When Adam sees the woman, he recognizes her immediately for the purpose she will have in his life, a helper to accomplish God's will for their service to Him, one whose femininity corresponds to his masculinity. His expression rendered often as "now at last" is in actuality indicative not of the end of a time-lengthy search, but rather as sudden discovery.[219]

There is ample evidence in the Scriptures outside of the book of Genesis that Adam and Eve were regarded by others as real individuals rather than simply mythical or allegorical figures. For instance, the apostle Paul considered them to be actual individuals as he makes his arguments about the entrance of sin into the world in Romans 5:12–21, in his arguments about the resurrection in 1 Corinthians 15:22–45, and in his arguments about church leadership in 1 Timothy 2:13–14. Luke includes Adam as an actual historical individual integral to the genealogy of Christ in Luke 3:34b–38. Jude, the half-brother of Jesus, regarded Adam as an individual in Jude 14. Jesus also considered them as real individuals as He discussed issues of marriage and divorce in Matt. 19:4–5. One can begin to see how the Scriptures begin to become unraveled as a truth source when one begins to deny the historicity of the Genesis narrative. I choose to believe the testimony consistent within the Scriptures both of the six-day creation and the historicity of the individuals Adam and Eve, based in a faith position in the authority of the Word of God written, insured by the Word of God incarnated, crucified, and resurrected.

Excursus: Too Much Happening on Day Six

[219] Though the term *happa'am* can mean the result of a long search in the Old Testament (as in Genesis 29:34–35; and Judg. 16:18, 28), the context of Genesis 1–2 suggests that of a sudden discovery (as in Ex. 9:27 and Judg. 15:3).

All of the activities that occur within a putative twenty-four-hour long sixth day concern many who are weighing the options of young earth versus old earth creation. On that sixth day, Scriptures reveals that quite of a number of things occurred, perhaps far too many when one considers all that was accomplished:

Genesis 1:24	God commanded the earth to generate land–based animals.
Genesis 1:25a	God made the land–based animals according to all their kinds.
Genesis 1:25b	God evaluated the animals and determined it was good.
Genesis 1:26	God deliberated (consulted with Himself) over the creation of man.
Genesis 1:27a & 2:7a	God fashioned man (as a potter fashions clay).
Genesis 2:7b	God breathes into man the breath of life.
Genesis 2:7c	Man becomes a living soul.
Genesis 2:8a	God *planted* (or, *had planted*) the garden of Eden.
Genesis 2:9	God made plants to grow out of the ground in the garden, including the Tree of Knowledge of Good and Evil and the Tree of Life.
Genesis 2:8b, 15	God placed the man in the garden to care for and keep the garden.
Genesis 2:16–17	God commanded the man not to eat from the Tree of Knowledge of Good and Evil.
Genesis 2:18	God evaluated the situation, determined it was not good that man should be alone, so planned to make a helper for Adam.
Genesis 2:19a	From the ground God forms all the beasts of the field and birds of the air.
Genesis 2:19b	God brings all the beasts of the field and birds of the air to Adam to see what Adam would name them.
Genesis 2:20a	Adam named all the cattle, birds of the sky, and beasts of the field
Genesis 2:20b	Adam realizes he lacks a helpmeet.
Genesis 2:21a	God put Adam into a deep sleep (anesthesia?).
Genesis 2:21b	God removes a rib from Adam's side (surgery with cutting, sewing, etc.?).
Genesis 1:27b, 2:22a	God built the woman from the flesh and bone of Adam.
Genesis 2:22b	God presents the woman to Adam.
Genesis 2:23a	Upon seeing the woman, Adam exclaims with great emotional intensity (as in cases elsewhere in Scripture where emotions have built up over a long time, such as Jacob's statement "now let me die" upon being reunited with his son Joseph after many years in Genesis 46:30).
Genesis 2:23b	Adam names the woman "Woman."
Genesis 1:28–30	God blessed the man and woman and invested them with dominion over the created order.
Genesis 1:31	God assessed everything that He had made (*i.e.* the entire universe) and evaluated it as "very good."

As one looks at this list, one may observe that the difficulties are not so much on the activities of the omnipotent God, who can accomplish His will at whatever speed He chooses, but rather on the time it would take for Adam to name "all" the cattle, birds, and beasts of the field. Because this issue causes many to stumble over the twenty-four-hour meaning for *yôm* in chapter 1,[220] it is therefore necessary to address it here.

If one understands the geographical context of the naming of the animals to be within the confines of the special garden that God had made and into which He had placed Adam, the "all" (or "every") seems to suggest only those animals that were included in that Garden. Could it not be that Adam named only that fauna concomitant with the garden itself, i.e., a limited amount of animals in an apparently somewhat confined space,[221] rather than all possible species that would eventually roam the entire globe?[222] (One remembers the blessing to be fruitful, multiply, and fill the earth.) Surely, if Adam were blessed with the faculties of a mind untainted by sin before the fall, it would not take him very long to recognize what God desired him to understand: it was not good for him to be alone and as yet, there was no helper suitable for him. This task could have been easily accomplished in a time far shorter than a twenty-four-hour day.

---

220 As an example, Miles V. Van Pelt has written: "Estimates of the number of species currently in existence range from two to one hundred million. How the man would have named even a fraction of these animals in a single day is well beyond comprehension." ("Exegetical Evidence for Non–Solar and Non–Sequential Interpretations of the Genesis 1 and 2 Creation Days," unpublished presentation, Evangelical Theological Society annual meeting, Providence, RI, Nov. 2008, 11).

221 The garden seemed to have had a gate or something akin to it, as it was later guarded (cf. Gen. 3:24).

222 This is not special pleading but rather an attempt to deal with the text as given and the context in which it is presented. These are basic tenets of traditional hermeneutics.

Eleven: Conclusion

For the sake of argument, let's review some of my initial comments. Let's take the virgin birth of Christ for a moment as an example of what can happen by yielding the Scripture to science. Since science normally understands parthenogenesis in humans to be biologically impossible, then employing a nonliteral hermeneutic to Matthew's gospel similar to that used by many in Genesis 1 would yield a discovery that Jesus was not indeed born of a virgin, but that He had a human father. The hypostatic union of fully God with fully Man in one person would then be lost.

As yet another example, let's look at the resurrection. Since scientific empirical data would yield the results that no one has ever risen from the dead, nor is likely to (other than resuscitations, which are temporary), then Jesus did not rise from the dead. The words of the Bible that describe this event, including the testimony of hundreds of eyewitnesses, cannot survive this modern grid. The resurrection itself would not be able to survive the warp of nonliteral hermeneutic nor the woof of scientific investigation. In other words, filtering Scripture through that particular grid work leaves nothing solid in which to believe.

Consider for a moment that which has already taken place in some scholarly religious circles with Genesis 2 and 3. Patricia Williams, an Episcopal priest, by comparing Scripture with published scientific data, has denied not only the historicity of Adam and Eve, but also the historicity of the fall of mankind into sin.[223] She maintains that Eve represents a female which would have been the first of the species of man, and that psychology affirms that man is innately good.[224] Both of these views, of course, directly oppose the clear teaching of the Scriptures.

Now, with science by implication having removed an all–powerful God from the creative process, having removed the historicity of Adam, Eve, the fall, the virgin birth of Christ, and having removed the resurrection, what is left for the Christian? Faith, only faith, they would maintain. To which I would reply: faith in what? Faith placed in a God who may or may not have started the creative process, and if He had, may have taken billions of years to complete it? Why would I fear such a God? Given enough time without decay and death, you or I might be able to do the same thing! Why should I believe in such an impotent God? Since there was no fall, no sin nature, then I have no reason to fear this God as I have no accountability to Him. Since Jesus was not virgin born, He was only a man, not God. And since He did not rise from the grave, what hope do any of us have, except perhaps in a false hope in a Santa Claus? A false hope that we would have in a fat, bearded, benevolent old man who will welcome us into eternity? Why, we don't even have any ancient books that would lead us to that conclusion!

The case is clear in my thinking, and I hope in yours. There does exist, metaphorically speaking, a line of dominoes that can be toppled if the first one falls. The one in the front, if felled, begins the toppling of all the rest. The assault of the Enemy is on the front piece of those dominoes: it is on the front of time, it is at the front of the Bible. If the front falls, a vibrant, living Christianity will eventually fall with it. An empty shell of real

[223] Patricia Williams, "Can Christianity Get Along Without Adam and Eve?" *Research News & Opportunities in Science and Religion* 3:3 (November 2002): 20.
[224] Ibid.

Christianity might continue to exist for a while, if people continue to choose to be inconsistent with their hermeneutics at best or willfully ignorant at worst, but the real Christianity will be lost.

Having said these things, it is most important to remember that we do not conduct our battle with humanity. Too, it is doubtful that anyone has been won to Christ by losing an argument to a Christian. Our battle is spiritual, as the apostle Paul says: "For our battle is not against flesh and blood, but against the rulers, against the powers, against the world forces of this darkness, against the spiritual forces of wickedness in the heavenly places."[225] It is enough for us to offer what the Bible clearly teaches, and to make plausible explanations of what sometimes may not seem so clear. It is therefore appropriate for us to teach that God is the Creator, that He created quickly and powerfully, and that we are responsible before Him. It is appropriate to teach that He gave Himself in the person of His Son Jesus, fully God and fully man, who offered Himself on Calvary as a payment for our sins, that He Himself might redeem us to God and take us to heaven.

Do not be deceived by those who would offer scientific observations as fact set against the very clear and authoritative words of the Bible regarding creation. They are those who view an old earth to be the only conclusion to be derived from their interpretation of the data obtained by modern empirical observations. Honest scientists, however, recognize that theories initially hypothesized can be disproven over time. They will normally admit that they are not the final word on a given subject. Those who refuse to do so would not be regarded as open-minded by this present author.[226] However, the same Bible has been

---

[225] Ephesians 6:12.
[226] No doubt such scientists would not recognize me as such, either!

teaching the same doctrine of creation for millennia without change, as given by the ultimate Author, who is the same yesterday, today, and forever.

Appendix A: The Framework Hypothesis

In the face of the seemingly insurmountable evidence of an old earth from modern empirical observations, many scholars have sought to interpret Genesis 1:1–2:3 in a way that harmonizes the elegant and clear words of the Scripture with popular scientific understanding. One of the most popular modern ways of thinking about this has yielded what is called by many the Framework hypothesis.

In a nutshell, the Framework hypothesis affirms a literary structure (or, framework) to the Genesis 1 account, which is built upon the terms *tōhû wāḇōhû* found in 1:2. With the understanding that these two terms may be glossed as "unformed and unfilled" or as "uninhabitable and uninhabited," many have suggested that these words set the structure, or framework, for the six creation days. Specifically, days 1–3 correct the untenable situation of being unformed while days 4–6 correct the uncomfortable situation of being unfilled.

For some, this possible structural indicator reflects the literary abilities of the narrator. For others it is simply a circumstantial observation. On the one hand, some see the structure but believe it does not lessen the normal understanding of the semantic meaning of the terms that build the passage. They would say that it is both literary and literal.[227] On the other hand, the very fact that such an overt structure exists (if indeed it does) may suggest that the words

[227] One should note both the literary and literal structure of Acts 1:8 at this point governs the structure of the entire book. Revelation 1:19 is thought by many to be a similar outline to that book.

in the passage should be understood as figures of speech, anthropomorphic words, as it were. Bruce Waltke has written that the six days of creation are twenty-four-hour days like ours but are also "metaphorical representations of a reality beyond human comprehension and imitation."[228] Though he affirms the passage is indeed a narrative, the language of Genesis 1 is "figurative, anthropomorphic, not plain."[229] As distinct from straightforward historical narrative, he says: "The text . . . is begging us not to read it in this way."[230] As such, literalness may not be in view in the light of such elegant literature. Miles Van Pelt takes it a bit further by suggesting that recognizing "the 'architectural' significance of Genesis 1:2 for the construction of the creation days is an important factor in properly interpreting the nature of these days."[231] I understand him to mean here that the presence of literary structure in 1:2 plays a significant role in determining the lexical meaning of words that follow.[232] The concept of six days was then adopted by Moses in Exodus 20:11 to form the workweek governed by the Shabbat (Sabbath), but otherwise may have no significance.

The Impetus behind the Development of the Framework Hypothesis

Modern empirical observations popularized by well–educated and articulate scientists obviously overwhelm us with the complexity, beauty, and grandeur of the heavens and earth. I am at times mesmerized by the wonderful photography provided by the Hubble telescope, or of the creatures of the deep on view at the Chattanooga and Gatlinburg aquariums. It is

---

[228] Bruce K. Waltke, "The Literary Genre of Genesis, Chapter 1," *Crux* 27:4 (1991): 8.

[229] Ibid., 7.

[230] Ibid., 6. Actually, the text is not begging at all. It is stating what happened.

[231] Miles Van Pelt, "Exegetical Evidence for Non–solar and Non–Sequential Interpretation of the Genesis 1 and 2 Creation Days," ETS, 2008, 2.

[232] Van Pelt declares on page five: "In Genesis 1:2, the presentation of days is identified as logical, not chronological," which statement had not been substantiated to that point of his argument or was it at any later point. In fact, the term "day" does not appear in 1:2; therefore he implies that the structure he observes in 1:2 changes the meanings not only of "day," as well as "evening and morning," but also the governing ordinal numbers. On the contrary, the description of the days from one to six do indeed reflect chronology, simply from the words in those verses if nothing else.

wonderful to view Planet Earth or the satellite images provided by Google. Many evangelical biblical scholars are also certainly enamored by such data. Recent emails from two scholars whom I consider my good friends (and thus will remain anonymous) demonstrate this point. One wrote and chided me for adhering to the traditional understanding of literal days: "I have to admit, however, that with all the apparent discontinuities between modern empirical observation of the cosmos (general revelation, if you will) and Genesis 1, I am surprised that you want to view the latter as scientific."[233] Still another wrote a more extreme position to me on Darwin's birthday in February 2009: "Darwinian Evolution is as certain as the resurrection of Christ." The former email comes from one who holds to the Framework hypothesis, so I was not surprised by his comments. However, I am just amazed at the second one's statement, since belief in the resurrection of Christ rests on faith by those who honor the Bible as God's authoritative Word on the subject. The same hermeneutic that holds to that belief is just as valid in Genesis 1. Despite this, yet another friend has recently publicly stated that "the when and the how of Genesis 1 are not important, the why and the Who are."[234] Though they would deny it, my friends have subconsciously bowed the knee to science.

Those holding the Framework hypothesis often appeal to portions of Genesis 1 and 2 which seem to be problematical for the traditional understanding to be upheld. It would be good for us to understand these reasons and to evaluate them in light of the biblical text.

There are basically three areas of great concern that lead some scholars to question the validity of Genesis 1 as reflecting the actual events of the creation week as revealed by

---

[233] My rejoinder to this is that I don't regard Genesis 1 to be scientific; I believe it to be a true literary yet literal account of what happened, given by revelation by God.

[234] Taped message recorded for Radio Broadcast, Fall 2014. I will not document this further at this time due to friendship considerations.

God. These are the issues of anthropomorphic days, the number of events on the sixth day that would mandate too much time for accomplishment, and the issue of light apart from the sun.

Anthropomorphic Days

In the Framework hypothesis the term "day," as well as the terms "evening and morning," would have no meaning in reality, but are rather "anthropomorphic" meant to be comprehensible to the primitive mind. Waltke poses the question:

> If the other panels in the process of creation are anthropomorphic representations of creation, is it not plausible to suppose the same is true of the chronological framework, the six days? God lisped so that Israel could mime him, working six days and resting the seventh (Exod. 20:11).[235]

Should we join hands in agreement with Dr. Waltke over this issue? In employing anthropomorphism and metaphor, it is important to realize the element of truth behind those figures of speech. When we are told that "God said," we may agree that God, who is spirit, does not have organs of speech as ours, but we would probably all agree that God is able to communicate. Likewise, "God heard" does not mandate organs of hearing but does indicate His ability to receive information as if He indeed had those auditory, cartilage filled extremities. The growing hot of the nose of God, idiomatic for His anger, does not require that God have a physical nose as ours. But does this require that the "days" of Genesis 1:1–2:3 be so understood? Young has pointed out that to so designate the "days" to be anthropomorphism is not tenable. He writes:

> . . . for the word anthropomorphism, if it is a legitimate word at all, can be applied to God alone and cannot properly be used of the six days . . . . If the days are to be

[235] Waltke, "The Literary Genre," 8.

> interpreted non–chronologically, the evidence for this must be something other than the presence of anthropomorphisms in the first chapter of Genesis.[236]

It seems to the present writer then that to name the days of Genesis 1 as anthropomorphic days has two implications. One, it violates the normally accepted definition of "anthropomorphism," which means to attribute to God human characteristics. Two, it violates the basic gloss of the word *day* in similar genres and in similar syntactical constructions found elsewhere in the Bible. To cling to such a perversion of meaning is to engage in special pleading.

The Activities of Day Six

Waltke is particularly concerned with the order and number of events that occurred on day six of the creation week, particularly in regard to the growth of the trees: "Unlike chapter 1, where one could appeal to apparent age with reference to such things as the stellar bodies, one cannot make a similar appeal to the planted trees . . . the Genesis narrative, using the verbs 'plant' and 'cause to grow,' gives no indication that an extraordinary quick growth of trees is intended."[237] It is true that the verbs themselves do not give us an indication of the speed of growth.[238] However, the examples given to us by the creation of Adam and Eve as mature adults and the creation of the best wine by Jesus at the wedding of Cana in John 2 grant at least some insight in the way God can produce apparent age in a very short period of time. Should we discount these narratives because science says such things are impossible? I think not. Regarding Adam naming "all" the animals, could it not be that perhaps Adam

---

[236] Edward J. Young, *Studies in Genesis 1*, 58.

[237] Waltke, "The Literary Genre," 7. It seems to the present writer that the apparent age of stellar bodies is a more difficult problem to a recent creation than that of the trees.

[238] My personal conception of the creation of flora that sprouted from the earth was similar to watching the blooming of a rose blossom with time lapse photography. By the end of the third day, vegetation was evident in every stage of maturity, but only less than a day old in chronological time. One wonders if the same might have been true with the speed of light.

named only that fauna concomitant with the garden itself, i.e., a limited amount of animals in a apparently somewhat confined space, rather than all possible species? Surely, if Adam were blessed with the faculties of a mind untainted by sin, it would not take him very long to recognize what God did: it was not good for him to be alone and as yet, there was no helper suitable for him.

Light Apart from the Sun

Waltke states: "the creation of light on the first day and of luminaries on the fourth, confirms our suspicion that Genesis 1 ought not be read as straightforward history."[239] He further asks: "How can there be three days characterized by day and night before the creation of the luminaries to separate the day from the night and to mark off the days? Are we clueless?"[240] This issue also troubles Van Pelt. He says that "the biblical text is unaware of such an explanation"[241] as to how this might be. Since physical light cannot exist apart from a physical sun, he says: "A logical conclusion from such a description is that days one and four describe the same events."[242] These statements may be met by appeal to *sensus plenor*, a Latin term that may be understood to mean "the meaning of all parts." There is ample evidence elsewhere in Scripture equating God Himself with the concept of light. Psalm 104:2 reveals that He cloaks Himself with light. Isaiah 60:19 informs Israel that they will ultimately have no need of the sun: "No longer will you have the sun for light by day, nor for brightness will the moon give you light; but you will have the Lord for an everlasting light, and your God for your glory" (NASV). First John 1:5 states that God is light. Revelation 21:23 indicates that in heaven, no sun is necessary, for it the glory of God Himself that illumines

239 Waltke, "The Literary Genre," 7.

240 Ibid. Actually, we are not clueless to believe the Scriptures that are clear that our God is able to bring forth light from Himself without the need for the sun (see discussion below).

241 Van Pelt, 4.

242 Ibid., 5.

the new earth where there is no darkness. Therefore with God present, as He surely was in Genesis 1, there is no need for a physical sun for light to exist. The citing of such passages in support of the plain reading of Genesis 1 is a normal part of a biblical hermeneutic which accepts the text as inspired and authoritative. Therefore, citing such is not to be derided as "special pleading" in the light of the "modern empirical observations" of scientific inquiry.[243]

Evaluation of the Literary Framework Hypothesis

In the most pervasive literary Framework hypothesis, the sequencing of days normally established in Hebrew by the presence of ordinal numbers is negated. They would have no meaning in reality but simply exist to serve as literary structural markers, serving the master framework established by 1:2.

In this extreme form of the Framework hypothesis, the jussives of command were not actually issued by God to His creation; they were not really fiat commands, nor were they responded to immediately to reflect the power of God's position and authority. They simply reveal metaphorically that God is in control, and thus are divested of normal meaning. But if metaphorical, who determines the meaning of the metaphor? Who is qualified to issue the final word? The statements of completion expressed by "and it was so" (*wayhî kēn*) then are only literary expressions, devoid of any factual meaning. Finally, the assessment that God gives on each day that it was "good" and finally that it was "very good" really would have no meaning whatsoever.

Finally, seeing artistic and literary structure in the creation account of Genesis 1 and 2 does not necessarily have to negate the traditional Christian understanding. It may rather reflect the literary beauty of which God must certainly be capable. However, when the

243 Indeed, traditional hermeneutics would relegate the findings of science near the outer regions of the appropriate interpretive steps.

literary Framework hypothesis gives dominant priority to the meaning and positioning of the terms *tōhû wāḇōhû* by ignoring the clear understanding of the remainder of the passage, there are problems. One is that the hypothesis itself in its most extreme form is built upon the supposition that the meanings of *tōhû wāḇōhû* are clear enough to build a theory on them that negates a traditional reading of the passage. It then not only negates the normal understanding of the meanings of the words of Genesis 1 and 2 but actually undermines the use of similar traditional hermeneutics in other parts of Scripture as well.

It is my considered opinion that when the Framework hypothesis invalidates the plain meaning of the words it governs, it is untenable. I see no plausible explanation for adopting such a concept other than a desire to be "academically acceptable" to the scientific community and to those biblical scholars so influenced by it. By doing this, scholars have abandoned the preeminence of the Scripture in matters of science, at the very least. The danger of such an abandonment of biblical authority was well expressed by Tennessee State Attorney General Thomas Stewart who prosecuted the Scopes Evolutionary Trial in Dayton, TN, in 1925:

> Yes, discard that theory of the Bible—throw it away, and let scientific development progress beyond man's origin. And the next thing you know, there will be a legal battle staged within the corners of this state, that challenges even permitting anyone to believe that Jesus Christ was divinely born—that Jesus Christ was born of a virgin—challenge that, and the next step will be a battle staged denying the right to teach that there was a resurrection, until finally that precious book and its glorious teachings upon which this civilization has been built will be taken from us.[244]

[244] *The Most Famous Court Trial*, 197–98. This certainly seems to have become the case as we have recently passed the year of the 150th anniversary of *Origin of Species*. The present writer had the privilege of portraying Thomas Stewart (later US Senator from Tennessee) in the annual reenactment of the actual trial transcript for over six years. The play was *Monkey in the Middle* by Gail Johnson, and was held in the actual original courtroom in Dayton, TN.

Appendix B: Theodicy, the Fossil Record, and God's Care for the Animals

Introduction

The fossil record clearly depicts predation, disease, suffering, and death in the animal kingdom. This record is interpreted differently by those who hold to a recent quick creation and those who believe that the creation actually occurred over millions of years.

Those who hold the former position (the "young earth" position) must explain the fossil record as being formed since the creation week. Though admitting the testimony of the fossil record regarding death, the young earth creationist insists that disease, suffering, and death in the animal kingdom all occurred as a result of judgment on the sin of man at the fall. Then and only then could the fossil record begin to be written. To state otherwise, i.e., to claim that God allowed such suffering gratuitously, would impugn the justice of God, or, to cite an analogy, to commit the sin of Job ("Will you charge Me with evil so that you may be righteous?" Job 40:8). Thus, such suffering could not have occurred before the fall of man logically, nor could it occur before the fall chronologically, since each creation day was said to be "good" (understood to preclude the possibility of death and decay), and the completion of that week "very good." Crucial issues then involve the questions of what is meant by the Hebrew term *ṭôb* "good," how the Bible defines death, and when death entered into the animal kingdom.

On the other hand, those who would hold to a progressive creation or a theistic evolution position (described as the "old earth" position) must answer those same questions differently. Goodness as depicted in the Hebrew word *ṭôb* must allow for death and decay. Death, disease, and suffering in the animal kingdom must have occurred chronologically before the fall of mankind into sin. Corollary to this second statement must be the understanding that Adam's sin introduced death only into the world of humanity, not into the entire creation. If this is indeed the case, death in the animal kingdom must have some other genesis. In one very real sense, and as was recently perhaps overstated to me by another Old Testament scholar, one must hold that "God does not care for the animals." Since the fossil record itself seems to bear testimony to millions of years, one must come to these or like conclusions in order also not to impugn the justice of God. This is the issue of theodicy.

To address these issues in a preliminary way, this appendix will initially examine the concept of *ṭôb* as found in the Old Testament Scriptures. Next, the author will offer some observations from Romans 5 and Romans 8 on the extent of death in the world as introduced by the sin of Adam.

In the second half of this appendix, the present writer will try to present a balanced observation of the biblical passages that reflect God's relationship with the animal kingdom. This will be done in order to determine principles that can inform our thinking on the issue at hand. In other words, if the Scriptures seem to indicate that God is really unconcerned about the animal kingdom, then the old earth perspective may have some credence, since our God is the same yesterday, today, and forever (Heb. 13:8). If, however, the Scriptures indicate that God does indeed care for the welfare of the animal kingdom, then the young earth understanding may be the correct one, since God *is* the same yesterday, today, and forever.

The Assessment of *ṭôb*

A perusal of the occurrences of *ṭôb* ('good" in the Hebrew Old Testament yields the following observation: Though there are many and various nuances to the adjective *ṭôb*, which are determined by context, none of those explicitly include the concept of death of any kind. Having said this, it must be admitted that a few of the occurrences seem to indicate that death is to be preferred over life in certain circumstances. This involves the adjective *ṭôb* with a comparative *min*, yielding the "better than" sayings. For instance, in his ironic despair over the success of his ministry, Jonah laments: "my death is better than my life" (Jonah 4:3; cf. 4:8 as he laments the loss of the sheltering plant). One could easily question Jonah's emotional state of mind from this statement. A second example may be found in Ecclesiastes 6:3, wherein Koheleth employs the same syntactical construction to indicate that a miscarried child is better than one who dies unsatisfied with life and then is improperly buried.[245] Neither of these two examples appears to be sufficient for one to explicitly equate death with the quality of being "good."

In fact, some uses of the word *ṭôb* indicate its close relationship with life rather than with death. In Deuteronomy 30:15, Moses challenges the people with the choice of obedience or disobedience to the covenant obligations when he says: "See, I have placed before you today life and good, or death and evil" (cf. Amos 5:14). This indicates in my thinking that the term "good" is more closely related to life than to death. Genesis 50:20 records Joseph's perspective on the providence of God when he reminds his brothers: "Though you planned evil against me, God planned it for good, in order to do as this day, to preserve the life of many people." Here, good involves the preservation of life rather than the

[245] Perhaps this should be construed as a comparison between two states of death rather than a contrast between life and death.

allowance of death. In 1 Kings 22, Ahab complains against the prophet Micaiah that he would not prophesy good to him but rather evil. That "evil" Micaiah ultimately announced involved the imminent death of Ahab in battle, so it seems to me that Ahab understood a good prophecy to include life and victory.

It seems to the present writer that the term *ṭôb* cannot be understood to have the death of man involved in any sense. Therefore, any claims of cruel animal predation, disease, and death before the fall of man into sin in Genesis 3 must have better evidence than simply disregarding the normal use of *ṭôb*.

Death in Romans 5

There is no question in my mind that the emphasis of Romans 5:12–21 regarding death focuses on human death and the possibility of redemption in Christ. It may be therefore that the apostle intended no word in this particular passage about death in the rest of the created order as a result of man's sin. James Stifler wrote: "The material creation was affected on account of Adam's sin (Genesis 3:17), but not by direct connection, and Paul does not contemplate it in the word 'world.' He means the world of mankind."[246] Alva McLain proclaimed: "God did not start out this world with death, as far as the human race is concerned."[247] On the other hand, the very passage in question begins with the phrase: *dia touto hōsper dia henos anthrōpou hē hamartia eis ton kosmon eisēlthen kai dia tēs hamartias ho thanatos*, "because of this, just as through one man sin entered into the world and through sin, death." Though the passage develops the concept of imputation of Adam's sin to the human race resulting in death, this initial phrase could be understood to refer to death

---

[246] James M. Stifler, *The Epistle to the Romans*, (Moody, 1960): 95.
[247] Alva McClain, *Romans: The Gospel of God's Grace*, ed. Herman A. Hoyt, (Moody, 1973): 135.

invading the entire created order, named here as the *kosmos*, a word commonly understood as referring to the ordered world created out of chaos. This viewpoint, however, is difficult to sustain from the usages of the term elsewhere in the Scriptures, wherein most cases humanity or the human world system is in view.[248] This fact seems to indicate that Paul did not have animal death in mind in Romans 5.

Corruption in Romans 8

Unlike Romans 5, wherein Paul focused on human death as a result of human sin, the wording of Romans 8 does seem to indicate that the fall of Adam brought decay to the created world. This decay, or corruption, is indicated by the term *phthora* in Romans 8:21. (This verse is commonly used in conjunction with Genesis 3:17ff to suggest that there were consequences imposed upon at least parts of creation due directly to Adam's wrong choice.)[249] The term *phthora* is used elsewhere in the New Testament to refer to the decay of the flesh. It is central for the apostle Paul as he teaches concerning the resurrection (1 Cor. 15:42, 50; cf. Gal. 6:8). Peter uses it to refer to the ultimate death and destruction of both the unrighteous and the animals (2 Pet. 2:12). In Romans 8, Paul teaches that it is the entire creation that has been subjected to futility, existing now in slavery to this corruption. He does not use *kosmos* but rather *ktisis*, creation, a word most normally including both man and animals. James Stifler writes: "This verse clearly implies that creation (all nature) is neither in its original condition nor in its final condition. It fell when man fell (Genesis 3:17–19); it shall be restored when he is, and shall be no longer subject to vanity, but to him (Heb. 2:5–

[248] Even in Acts 17:24, the term is separated from the phrase "and all things in it." Cf. J. Guhrt, "κοσμος," in *The New International Dictionary of New Testament Theology*, edited by Colin Brown, (Zondervan, 1986): 1:524.

[249] William Sanday and Arthur C. Headlam, *Romans*, International Critical Commentary, fifth edition, (Edinburgh: T&T Clark, 1902): 207.

9).”[250] Decaying corruption then was brought into the creation through the agency of Adam’s sin (and some would say through the representative participation of the animal kingdom in the temptation by the serpent). This would seem to preclude the possibility of death and its resulting decay before the fall, if the introduction of that death and decay came as a result of the fall.[251]

Examples in Scripture of Animal Death Resulting from Man’s Sin

There are examples offered in Scripture where animals died as a result of the sin of man. Though not explicitly stating that an animal died to provide the raw material for the skin tunics God made for Adam and Eve, Genesis 3:21 strongly implies this sacrifice of death as covering (atonement) for their sin. To suggest that God simply “created” the skins separate from the death of a living animal may testify of His power, but it seems to be special pleading. One may ask at this point: “How can a just God who cares about animals allow one to die as a result of man’s sin?” It is because He cares more about man as the crown of His creation, and as His representative to the created order, that He allows a substitute to pay the penalty as an atonement, or covering over, for man’s sin. In so doing, the sacrificed animal becomes the foreshadowing of His ultimate sacrifice in the person of His own Son, the ultimate redeemer for our sins (“the lamb of God, slain before the foundation of the world”).

A clearer example comes in the flood account. In Genesis 6:5, we read that “the evil of man was great on the earth, and every intent of the thoughts of his heart was only evil all day long.” Genesis 6:12 concurs with “it was corrupted, for all flesh had corrupted its way upon the earth.” Out of His grief concerning man, He planned to blot out all mankind by

---

[250] Stifler, 144.

[251] Recent suggestions that the cruel animal death occurred long before man’s sin, but anticipated it, appears to this writer to be special pleading in an attempt to harmonize evolutionary theory with theology.

means of the waters of the flood. Those creatures not having access to the ark would of course perish alongside of humanity. Culpability in the animal kingdom is not stressed, though some might argue that it did exist in some way.[252] It is the gross sinfulness of man that was bringing about the destruction.

A strong example comes in the entire Levitical system of animal sacrifice. Bulls, sheep, goats, and certain birds died as atoning sacrifices not only for the sinfulness of individual men but also as part of the daily cult sacrifices on behalf of the community.

God's Care for the Animals

There are a number of passages that deal directly with God's watch care of the animal kingdom, and some others wherein that concern is strongly implied. These will be dealt with in the discussion below.

The Flood (*mabbûl*) of Noah (Genesis 6–9)

Taking either a global or a local view of the flood of Noah,[253] the one who would hold to narrative truth would have to admit that the ark provided a means of preserving both human and animal life. That God is interested in the preservation of a remnant of the animal kingdom during the great flood is made clear by Genesis 6:19–20. He informs Noah that "two of every kind shall come to you to keep them alive." That He intends this rescue to

[252] Perhaps the later concept of *ḥerem* would inform one's thinking at this point. When a city was under total *ḥerem*, the men, women, children, and animals would all be slain, and the city burned with fire (cf. Josh. 8:18–19, 1 Sam. 15:3; though at times the animals could be taken as spoil, cf. Josh. 11:14) . It was to be a total judgment, not only of sinners but on all they associated with. A similar idea may be found in Leviticus 16:16 when on the Day of Atonement, the altar and the tabernacle itself needed the sprinkling of blood for atonement, because of the proximity of sinful men who served there.

[253] The normal Hebrew word for a local flood, and not found in Genesis 6–9, is *šeṭep*. Outside of Genesis 6–9, the great *mabbûl* of Noah's history is mentioned only once again, in Psalm 29:10.

ensure propagation may be seen in the words "keep offspring alive on the face of the earth" (Gen. 7:2–3).

Much may be made of the use of the verb *zākar* in Genesis 8:1: "But God remembered Noah and every living thing and every animal with him in the ark." Westermann states:

> "Remember" in this context implies mercy toward the one threatened with death. At the same time it introduces the saving action (so too Ex 2:24). God's merciful remembrance "extends in a touching way even to the animals in the ark" (H. Holzinger); some interpreters refer to Jonah 4:11.[254]

Exodus

One observes in the book of the covenant (Exod. 20–24) specific instructions given for Israel's obedience to God. Though the Sabbath was mentioned earlier in the Decalogue, one purpose of it is found in the book of the covenant in Exodus 23:12: "Six days you shall do your work, but on the seventh day you shall cease, in order that your bull and your donkey may rest, and the son of your maidservant and the stranger may refresh themselves." In this case, it is not only the existence of the animal that is central, it seems that their quality of life is enhanced somewhat by this rest.

Deuteronomy

Deuteronomy 22:4 informs us that even animals belonging to others are important when it says "you shall not see the donkey of your brother or his bull falling on the road and hide yourself from them; you will surely raise *them* up with him." It is difficult to say conclusively that the emphasis should be placed on the animal's life or on the usefulness such an animal would have for the individual owner as moveable property (*miqneh*). Perhaps emphasis should be placed on one's responsibility to love one's neighbor as one loves

[254] Klaus Westermann, *Genesis 1–11*, (Fortress Press, 199): 441.

oneself (cf. Lev. 19:18). In any case, the animal has at least some importance, in that this regulation serves as one of the specific stipulations of the covenant obligation of Israel before God.

This idea of perpetuation of a species may be understood in Deuteronomy 22:6–7, regarding finding birds in a field: "you shall not take the mother with the young; you shall certainly let the mother go, but the young you may take for yourself, in order that it may be well with you and that you may prolong your days." The mother's continuance is necessary for the survival of the species, and as such her life is to be respected and preserved.

In some passages, God emphasizes provision for the animals. Deuteronomy 25:4 is classic in this regard: "You shall not muzzle your ox while he is threshing." The citation of the passage by the apostle Paul in 1 Corinthians 9:9 was meant to serve as an illustration of the necessity for properly providing for those engaged in ministry of the gospel. His statement: "God is not concerned about oxen, is He?" must be taken in the context in the comparative sense that God is more concerned about His own children engaged in His work than He is about beasts of burden (cf. 1 Cor. 9:14).

Psalms

Psalm 36:6–7 affirms that God's preservation of the life of man and animals is consistent with His covenant faithfulness: "O Lord, your loyal love is in the heavens, and your faithfulness as far as the skies; your righteousness is like the mighty mountains, your judgment like the great deep, man and beast you will deliver, O Lord." Why mention the deliverance of the beasts if they are not important to God?

In the great creation/flood poem that is Psalm 104, there are a number of verses that indicate God's provision for His animal creatures. The mountain springs created by God quench the thirst of the wild animals (104:11). He causes grass to grow for the cattle (104:14). The trees He has made provide homes for the birds, as do the rocks of the mountains for the goats and badgers (104:16–18). Young lions seek their food from God (104:21). He feeds the sea creatures to their satisfaction (104:28). Are we to understand these as literal truths reflective within a poetical passage, or simply as the poet's theological attribution to YHWH of what is seen in nature?

Jonah

Jonah 4:11 provides yet another example of God's care for the animals when He queries Jonah about his disappointment with the repentance of the Ninevites and with the withering of the sheltering plant: "Should I not have compassion over Nineveh, the great city, in which there is more than twelve ten–thousands of mankind who do not know between the right hand and the left; and many animals?" Not only is God concerned for the humanity of Nineveh but also for the animals.

Gospels

Jesus states a similar idea in the Sermon on the Mount. "Look at the birds of the air, that they do not sow, neither do they reap, nor gather into barns, and yet your heavenly Father feeds them. Are you not worth much more than they?" (Matt. 6:26). Man as the image of God representing God to the created order is more important than the birds, but that fact does not mitigate God's care for His other creatures. Luke 13:15 and 14:5 both affirm in a sense that the life of one's animal supersedes the prohibition against working on the Sabbath. "Does not each of you on the Sabbath untie his ox or his donkey from the stall, and lead him away to water him?" (13:15). One might think that the animal's comfort would be in view with this passage! "Which one of you shall have a son or an ox fall into a well, and will not immediately pull him out on a Sabbath day?" (14:5).

Reasonable Implications of God's Care for the Animals

One of the purposes of the creation of man was that he "rule" over the creation which God had made, specifically over the fish, fowl, land animals, and creeping things (Genesis 1:26–27). The word "rule" (*rādâ*) means to govern a dominion rightly established by God (Pss. 49:14; 110:2; 1 Kings 4:24; Isa. 41:2).[255] Adam begins to exercise this authority when he names the animals of the garden, thus showing dominion over them (Genesis 2:19–20). In part, this dominion may be what is meant by the image (*ṣelem*) of God. The term, when not associated with man, normally indicates idols, which simply function as representatives of the deity being worshiped (Num. 33:52; 2 Kings 11:18; Amos 5:26; cf. Dan. 2:31–35; 3:1–18).[256] In fact, one may understand the *bêt* preposition as a *bêt* of essence (translating "as" rather than "in" the image of God).[257] One of the divinely established purposes of mankind then as the image and likeness of God was to exercise authority over the created order as God's representatives.[258] To aver that God did not care for the animals prior to the creation of man seems to invalidate this purpose for man's existence.

---

[255] David M. Fouts, "Genesis 1–11," *Bible Knowledge Key Word Study*, ed. by Eugene H. Merrill, Victor Press, 2003, 1:44.

[256] Ibid., 1:43.

[257] Allen P. Ross, *Creation and Blessing*, Baker, 1988, 112.

[258] Scripture seems to apply to birds, fish, land animals, etc., the attributes of "blood," "flesh," "spirit," and "soul." Apparently only man has the added principle of the breath of God (*nᵉšāmâ*, Genesis 2:7). Man is therefore uniquely distinguished from the animal kingdom in that he is the image of God and he alone has the breath of God. Yet, he will perish in a manner similar to the animals (Eccl. 3:18–20).

In Proverbs 12:10, we are told that "A righteous man (*ṣaddîq*) has regard (*yādaʿ*) for the life of his beast." Since God is perfectly righteous, would one not also expect Him to care for the life of His beasts? God's righteousness is part of His immutable nature. If He is indeed concerned for His creatures in the post–fall world, it seems that He must also have been concerned in the pre–fall world.

Concluding Remarks

It seems to be clear from the Scripture that God is most concerned about humanity. However, sprinkled throughout the holy pages are clear statements that express the truth that God does care for the animal kingdom, which He created for His own glory. It is also true that animals do suffer disease, predation, and death as a result of the sin of man, and even forfeit their lives as temporary atonement for that sin. To suggest that God did not care for the animals before the fall as He clearly does afterward in a fallen world seems to argue against the very nature of our unchangeable God.

Index of Authors

Index of Topics

Index of Hebrew and Greek Words

Bibliography

Anderson, Bernhard W. *Out of the Depths*. Westminster, 1983.

Archer, Gleason L. *Encyclopedia of Bible Difficulties.* Zondervan, 1982.

Arnold, Bill T. *Encountering the Book of Genesis*. Baker, 1998.

Brueggemann, Walter. *Genesis*. Interpretation. John Knox Press, 1973.

Cassuto, Umberto. *A Commentary on the Book of Genesis: Part One: From Adam to Noah*. Magnes Press, 1961.

________. *The Documentary Hypothesis*. Magnes Press, 1961.

Coats, George W. *Genesis, with an Introduction to Narrative Literature*. Vol. 1 of Rolf Knierim and Gene M. Tucker, eds. Forms of the Old Testament Literature. Eerdman's, 1983.

Collins, C. John. "How Old is the Earth? Anthropomorphic Days in Genesis 1:1–2:3." *Presbyterion* 20/2 1994.

Fields, Weston W. *Unformed and Unfilled.* Burgerner Enterprises, 1976.

Fouts, David M. "How Short an Evening and Morning?" *CENTech Journal* 11:3 (1997): 307–8.

________. "A Defense of the Hyperbolic Interpretation of Large Numbers in Old Testament." *Journal of the evangelical Theological Society* 40 (1997): 377–87.

________. "Response Two to 'How Long an Evening and Morning.'" *Creation Ex Nihilo Technical Journal* 11:3 (1997): 303–4.

________. and Kurt Wise. "Blotting Out and Breaking Up: Miscellaneous Hebrew Studies in Geocatastrophism." In the *Proceedings of the Fourth International Conference on Creationism: Technical Symposium Sessions*. Edited by Robert E. Marsh. ICC (1998): 217–28.

Garrett, Duane. *Rethinking Genesis*. Mentor. Ross–shire, Great Britain, 2000.

Geisler, Norman L. *Baker Encyclopedia of Christian Apologetics*. Zondervan, 1999.

George, A. R. *The Babylonian Gilgamesh Epic: Introduction, Critical Edition and Cuneiform Texts*. Oxford, University Press, 2003.

Gibson, J. C. L. *Canaanite Myths and Legends*. T&T Clark, 1977.

Guhrt, J. "κοσμος." In *The New International Dictionary of New Testament Theology*. Edited by Colin Brown. Zondervan, 1986.

Hasel, Gerhard F. "The Significance of the Cosmology of Genesis I in relation to Ancient Near Eastern Parallels." *Andrews University Seminary Studies* 10 (1972): 1–20.

Hendel, Ronald. *The Text of Genesis 1–11*. Oxford, 1998.

Herdner, Andrée. *Corpus des tablettes en cunéiformes alphabétique.* Paris: Paul Guenther, 1963.

Johnston, Gordon H. "Genesis 1 and Ancient Egyptian Creation Myths." *Bibliotheca Sacra* 165 (2008):178–94.

Lambdin, Thomas O. *Introduction to Biblical Hebrew*. Scribner's, 1971.

Lewis, C. S. *The Magician's Nephew*. Collier, 1970.

McClain, Alva. *Romans: The Gospel of God's Grace*. Ed. by Herman A. Hoyt. Moody, 1973.

Mitchell, T. C. "The Old Testament Usage of Nešāma." *Vetus Testamentum* 11 (1961): 177–87.

Rooker, Mark F. "Genesis 1:1–3: Creation or Re–Creation? Part 1." *Bibliotheca Sacra* 149 (1992) 316–23; "Part 2." *Bibliotheca Sacra* 149 (1992) 411–27.

Ross, Allen P. *Creation and Blessing*. Baker, 1988.

________. *Introducing Biblical Hebrew*. Baker, 1999.

Ross, Hugh. *A Matter of Days*. NavPress, 2004.

________. *Creation and Time*. NavPress, 1994.

________. *The Fingerprint of God.* Second Edition. Reasons to Believe, 1991.

Roth, Wolfgang M. W. "The Numerical Sequence x/x+1 in the Old Testament." *Vetus Testamentum* 12 (1962): 300–311.

Sailhamer, John. *The Pentateuch as Narrative*. Zondervan, 1992.

Sanday, William and Arthur C Headlam. *Romans*. International Critical Commentary. Fifth edition. Edinburgh: T&T Clark, 1902.

Sarna, Nahum. *Understanding Genesis*. Schocken Books, 1970.

Sayce, A. H. "The Egyptian Background of Genesis 1." In *Studies Presented to F. Ll. Griffith.* London: Egypt Exploration Society (1932): 419–23.

Schottroff, Luise. "The Creation Narrative: Genesis 1.1–2.4a." In *A Feminist Companion to Genesis*. Sheffield, 1993.

Sternberg, Meir. *The Poetics of Biblical Narrative*. Indiana U. Press, 1985.

Stifler, James M. *The Epistle to the Romans*. Moody, 1960.

The World's Most Famous Court Trial. Original Transcript of the Scopes Trial. 2nd Reprint edition. Dayton, TN: Bryan College, 1990.

Tsumura, David T. "Genesis and Ancient Near Eastern Stories of Creation and Flood: An Introduction." In *I Studied Inscriptions from Before the Flood*. Ed. by Richard S. Hess and David Toshio Tsumura. Eisenbraun's, 1994.

Van Pelt, Miles V. "Exegetical Evidence for Non–Solar and Non–Sequential Interpretations of the Genesis 1 and 2 Creation Days." Unpublished presentation. Evangelical Theological Society annual meeting. Providence, RI, Nov. 2008.

Van Wolde, E. J. "The Text as an Eloquent Guide: Rhetorical, Linguistic and Literary Features in Genesis 1." Iin *Literary Structure and Rhetorical Strategies in the Hebrew Bible*. Eisenbraun's, 1996.

Waltke, Bruce K. *Genesis: a Commentary*. Zondervan, 2001.

________. "Barriers to Accepting the Possibility of Creation by Means of an Evolutionary Process." *Biologos* (biologos.org/uploads/projects/Waltke_scholarly_essay.pdf): 1–10.

________. *Creation and Chaos*. Portland: Western Seminary Press, 1974.

________. "The Literary Genre of Genesis, Chapter 1." *Crux* 27:4 (1991).

________ and M. O'Connor. *An Introduction to biblical Hebrew Syntax*. Eisenbraun's, 1990.

Walton, John H. *Ancient Israelite Literature in its Cultural Context*, Regency/Zondervan, 1989.

Westermann, Claus. *Genesis 1–11: A Continental Commentary.* Trans. by John J. Scullion. Fortress, 1994.

________. *Praise and Lament in the Psalms*. John Knox, 1981.

Whybray, R. N. *The Making of the Pentateuch*. JSOT Press, 1987.

Williams, Patricia. "Can Christianity Get Along Without Adam and Eve?" *Research News &*

Opportunities in Science and Religion 3:3 (November 2002).

Williams, Pete J. "What Does *min* Mean?" *CENTech Journal* 11:3 (1997): 344–52.

Williams, Ronald J. *Hebrew Syntax, An Outline*. 2nd ed. U. of Toronto, 1976.

Wiseman, P. J. *New Discoveries in Babylonia about Genesis*. 1936.

Young, Edward J. *Studies in Genesis 1*. An International Library of Philosophy and Theology: Biblical and Theological Studies. Ed. by J. Marcellus Kik. Presbyterian and Reformed, 1976.

Youngblood, Ronald. "The Days of Genesis 1: Anarthrous and Chronological/Non-chronological." Unpublished presentation at the Evangelical Theological Society. San Diego, Nov. 2007.

71722042R00096

Made in the USA
Columbia, SC
03 June 2017